THE
B ERING SEA AND
AL EUTIAN ISLANDS
RE GION OF WONDERS

Written by Terry Johnson
Edited by Kurt Byers
SG-ED-42

Alaska Sea Grant College Program
University of Alaska Fairbanks

Elmer E. Rasmuson Library Cataloging in Publication Data:

Johnson, Terry Lee, 1947-
The Bering Sea and Aleutian Islands : region of wonders / written by Terry Johnson ; edited by Kurt Byers. –
[Fairbanks, Alaska : Alaska Sea Grant College Program, University of Alaska Fairbanks], 2003.

p. : ill. ; cm. + 1 CD. - (Alaska Sea Grant College Program ; SG-ED-42)

Includes bibliographical references.

1. Bering Sea Region—Description and travel. 2. Bering Sea—Environmental aspects. 3. Aleutian Islands
(Alaska) —Description and travel. 4. Marine animals—Bering Sea. 5. Bering Sea Region—Economic conditions.
6. Bering Sea—Geography. 7. Fisheries—Bering Sea. 8. Bering Sea—History. I. Title. II. Johnson, Terry Lee,
1947-. III. Byers, Kurt. IV. Series: Alaska Sea Grant College Program ; SG-ED-42.

F951.J64 2003

ISBN 1-56612-081-0

Printed in China

Credits

Work for this book was supported by North Pacific Marine Research Program grant no. 124, a University of
Alaska federally funded program, through U.S. Geological Survey grant 99HQGR0103.

Publisher of the book is the Alaska Sea Grant College Program, which is cooperatively supported by the
U.S. Department of Commerce, NOAA National Sea Grant Office, grant no. NA16RG2321, projects A/161-01
and A/151-01; and by the University of Alaska Fairbanks with state funds. University of Alaska is an affirmative
action/equal opportunity institution. The views expressed herein do not necessarily reflect the views of the above
organizations.

Sea Grant is a unique partnership with public and private sectors combining research, education, and
technology transfer for public service. This national network of universities meets changing environmental and
economic needs of people in our coastal, ocean, and Great Lakes regions.

Cover design by Kurt Byers. Front cover photos: globe D. Coccia©; right, top down—Russell Hopcroft/UAF
and Kevin Raskoff/MBARI©, Alison Hammer©, Fred Hirschmann©, Kurt Byers/UAF©, Alissa Crandall©. Back
cover top, left to right—Mandy Merklein©, Brenda Konar/UAF©, U.S. Air Force©, Alison Hammer©; second
row—UC Santa Cruz Research Cruise©, Verena A. Gill©, Tony Lara©, Alison Hammer©, Tom Kline©. Table
of contents photos, top down, Alison Hammer©, Kurt Byers/UAF©, Fred Hirschmann©, U.S. Air Force©, Alissa
Crandall©, Stephen Jewett/UAF©, Russell Hopcroft/UAF and Kevin Raskoff/MBARI©.

Alaska Sea Grant College Program
University of Alaska Fairbanks
P.O. Box 755040
Fairbanks, Alaska 99775-5040
Toll free (888) 789-0090
(907) 474-6707 Fax (907) 474-6285
http://www.uaf.edu/seagrant/

TABLE OF CONTENTS

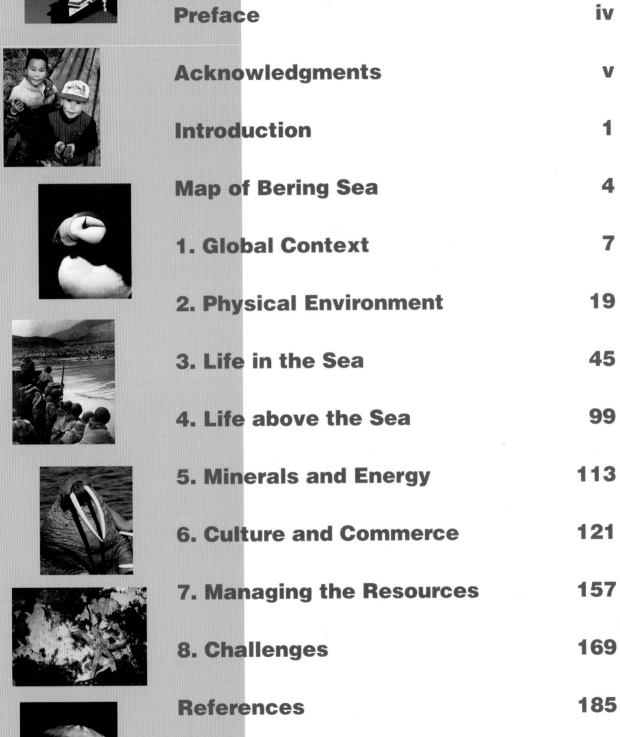

PREFACE

We wonder how many people not involved with marine issues can, without hesitation, point to the Bering Sea on a globe? We didn't do a survey to find out, but whatever the number, we expect this book will raise public awareness about a remarkable part of our planet.

While the Bering Sea may not occupy a top spot in most people's consciousness, it is an important place. And for people whose business it is to be aware of the Bering Sea, they are seeing major changes in the ecosystem.

Of course, in the grand view there is no such thing as a "normal" environment. The earth is a dynamic place. It's always changing. Indeed, change itself is the thing that's "normal" about natural earth systems. But as the human population and industrialization has grown, it's clear that humans are playing an increasingly significant role, influencing the environment faster than Nature can absorb and accommodate the effects of our residency.

As the Bering Sea signals problems due to accelerated environmental change, scientists are beginning the daunting task to sort out why things are changing and to what extent human activities are factors.

But why should we care about the Bering Sea? For one thing, Alaska's waters yield about half of the United States' annual seafood production. The majority of that comes from the Bering Sea and along the Aleutian archipelago.

Alaska and Russian coastal communities heavily depend on marine fisheries.

When fisheries suffer, so do the region's people. Most hurt are the thousands of Native subsistence users on the U.S. and Russian coasts who depend on marine species for food and trade. They have meager cash economies and few, if any, alternatives.

Downturns in the commercial fishing industry—which seesaws with the visitor industry as Alaska's second most valuable private industry next to oil extraction—unravels the socioeconomic fabric of rural communities. And the adverse effects don't stop with Alaska's remote villages—they ripple across the entire state.

The strength of Alaska's visitor industry with its recreational fishing, coastal sightseeing, and ecotour components also depends on a vibrant marine environment.

Perhaps the most fundamental reason to care about what is happening in the Bering Sea is the ethical responsibility we shoulder to be good stewards of the earth's environment.

Marine research

It is difficult to manage resource use for long-term sustainability if managers do not have reliable information about what's going on in the ecosystem. To get more good information, the U.S. Congress in 1999 established the North Pacific Marine Research Program (NPMR). The University of Alaska Fairbanks (UAF) School of Fisheries and Ocean Sciences (SFOS) was chosen to administer the $6.6 million program.

A primary objective of NPMR was to employ scientific muscle to "increase understanding of the Bering Sea," with the ultimate goal of improving the use and conservation of its resources. Results of NPMR science have been reported in science journals, technical publications, and conferences which convey the valuable information to scientists and resource managers.

Another objective of NPMR was to extend information about what is going on in the Bering Sea and the North Pacific to non-scientists—commercial fishermen, subsistence users, and the public at large. This book and radio program package addresses that objective.

Explore more

Creating this book was itself an adventure. The ink is hardly dry and I'm already looking forward to developing a second edition. All of us who worked on this book hope that it spurs interest in learning more about the history, culture, and environment of the Bering Sea region. We also hope that increased awareness will translate to better stewardship.

To extend your journey of discovery, visit the Alaska Sea Grant Web site at www.uaf.edu/seagrant, where you will find more resources on Alaska's seas and coasts, including many links to credible sources used to create this book.

—*Kurt Byers*
Editor

ACKNOWLEDGMENTS

Author

Terry Johnson

Terry Johnson lives in Homer, Alaska, and is a Marine Advisory Program (MAP) agent and faculty member with the University of Alaska Fairbanks (UAF) School of Fisheries and Ocean Sciences (SFOS). He authored the seminal book on commercial fishing in Alaska, *Ocean Treasure: Commercial Fishing in Alaska,* published by Alaska Sea Grant (ASG) in 2003. His writing appears in other MAP/ASG publications and in the commercial fishing trade press.

Johnson was a journalist in the U.S. Marine Corps, and holds a B.A. in communications and an M.A. in marine resource management, both from the University of Washington, Seattle.

Johnson spent a decade as MAP agent in Dillingham on Bristol Bay prior to assignment to Homer. He has taken many trips to the Russian Far East and Japan to study the seafood industry, and he lectures on that topic at UAF.

Johnson also is an advisor to the Alaska commissioners of the Pacific States Marine Fisheries Commission, and is a charter member of the Alaska Marine Conservation Council board of directors, a citizen's group that pursues sustained use and conservation of Alaska's marine resources.

Johnson has fished commercially throughout Alaska, including chasing salmon and herring in Bristol Bay and salmon on the Yukon River and in Norton Sound. He still keeps an oar in the water operating an ecotour charter out of Dillingham in the summer.

Architect

Kurt Byers, communications manager with ASG, housed in UAF/SFOS, conceived this book and radio project, proposed it to the North Pacific Marine Research Program (NPMR), and led the project to completion. Byers also edited the text, designed the book, shot photos, researched and selected photos and illustrations, wrote captions and some of the Sea Science sidebars, and provided relentless encouragement to the author.

Inspiration

Several years prior to establishment of NPMR, Richard Steiner, MAP agent and professor with UAF/SFOS, urged ASG to produce a book about the Bering Sea. The chapter subjects and much of their content reflect Steiner's vision. Steiner always seems to be a few steps ahead of the crowd, for one reason or another.

Radio stories

Douglas Schneider, information officer and radio producer with ASG, produced the radio stories about the NPMR studies that are on the compact disk packaged with this book. (If the disk is missing, contact ASG for a replacement or download the stories from the ASG Web site.) The stories originally were broadcast on Alaska Public Radio and other national and international outlets as part of ASG's Arctic Science Journeys radio series. Schneider also wrote some Sea Science sidebars and reviewed the text.

Photos and figures

This book features photos from some of Alaska's best outdoor photographers—Alissa Crandall, Fred Hirschmann, Tony Lara, Marion Owen, and Art Sutch.

Alissa Crandall's photos have appeared in *Outdoor Photographer, National Wildlife, Popular Photography, National Geographic World,* and other national publications. Her calendar credits include National Audubon Society, Sierra Club, World Wildlife Fund, National Wildlife Federation, and The Nature Conservancy. She has published four books, including *Paradise of the North: Alaska's Prince William Sound.* Crandall lives in Anchorage.

Fred Hirschmann's credits include numerous national calendars and magazines, including *Alaska, Newsweek, LIFE, National Geographic, National Wildlife, Outdoor Photographer,* and *Outside.* He is author and photographer of fifteen exhibit format books, including *Alaska from the Air, Alaska's National Parks,* and *Bush Pilots of Alaska.* Hirschmann lives in Wasilla.

Tony Lara fished for Bering Sea crab for 14 years and longlined for halibut. His photos often have been featured on covers and inside commercial fishing magazines and other publications, including *Alaska* and *Reader's Digest.*

Many of Lara's photos appear in the book *Ocean Treasure: Commercial Fishing in Alaska.* Lara lives in Kodiak.

Marion Owen is a former seaman and merchant marine officer turned photographer and organic gardener. Her photos and writing have appeared in national magazines including *National Wildlife* and *Alaska,* and are featured in a new book, *Kodiak: Alaska's Emerald Isle.* She also wrote the book, *Chicken Soup for the Gardener's Soul,* and with her husband operates a gourmet dinner cruise on Kodiak Harbor. Owen lives in Kodiak.

Art Sutch is a former Alaska commercial fisherman. A PADI and NAUI certified dive master, he operates a photography business and a dive charter company in Juneau. Schooled in photography and film, his images have been published in numerous publications and displayed as photo murals in aquariums and natural history centers.

In addition to Alaska-based photographers, we also include fine images from two photographers who can claim "honorary" Alaska citizenship—Mandy Merklein and Natalie Fobes. Both live in Washington state.

Mandy Merklein worked aboard Alaska commercial fishing and research vessels as a biologist, observer, and fisherman for over 20 years, much of that on the Bering Sea. As a state and federal fisheries observer, she worked on 80 boats in 10 different fisheries. Her photographs have been published internationally in books, magazines, newspapers, professional journals, and guidebooks, including *Neptune's Table: A View of America's Ocean Fisheries.*

Natalie Fobes' credits shine with five spreads in *National Geographic,* including one on the Bering Sea and two on the *Exxon Valdez* oil spill. She was nominated for a Pulitzer Prize in writing, and her books include *Reaching Home: Pacific Salmon, Pacific People,* and *I Dream Alaska.* More of Fobes' photos are featured in Johnson's book, *Ocean Treasure: Commercial Fishing in Alaska.*

In addition to the professional photographers, we extend thanks to all the other University of Alaska Fairbanks scientists, graduate students, and staff; government scientists, journalists, and others who contributed photographs, free of charge, recorded in the course of their work in laboratories and in the field.

Boat, fish, whale illustrations

Most of the fish and invertebrate illustrations were rendered by Sandra Noel, of Vashon Island, Washington. Noel is a former NOAA fisheries biologist. Her illustrations originally were created for use on harbor interpretive signs developed by ASG for installation at Ketchikan, Wrangell, and Seward, Alaska, and for use in the book, *Ocean Treasure: Commercial Fishing in Alaska.*

Noel's pen-and-ink line drawings were colored by Fairbanks, Alaska, artist, Lisa Peñalver. Peñalver also drew the razor clam, snow crab, and yellowfin sole.

Robert Hitz of Seattle drew the boats, which were colored by Peñalver. Like Noel's drawings, the boats originally were created for use with the Alaska harbor signs and in *Ocean Treasure: Commercial Fishing in Alaska.*

The cetacean illustrations were rendered by Garth Mix of Bellingham, Washington. Mix created the marine mammal drawings in *Guide to Marine Mammals and Turtles of the U.S. Atlantic and Gulf of Mexico,* coauthored by Kate Wynne of MAP and Malia Schwartz of Rhode Island Sea Grant. The book won the 2000 National Outdoor Book Award for best nature guidebook.

Maps

Some of the maps in this book were reproduced, with permission, from *Alaska in Maps,* an atlas published jointly by UAF, the Alaska Department of Education, and the Alaska Geographic Alliance. We thank Roger Pearson, co-editor of *Alaska in Maps* and UAF professor emeritus of geography, for his assistance and encouragement.

Other maps were reproduced, with permission, from *Ecoregions of the Bering Sea,* jointly published by the World Wildlife Fund and The Nature Conservancy of Alaska.

ASG graphic artist, Tatiana Piatanova, adapted the borrowed maps for use in this book, and created other maps and figures.

UAF Rasmuson Library

Like the gold discovered on the Seward Peninsula in 1888, the editor found a mother lode of historical images and original documents at the University of Alaska Fairbanks Elmer E. Rasmuson Library, Alaska and Polar Regions Department. Caroline Atuk-Derrick, library assistant, provided valuable guidance that led to uncovering the extraordinary original historical documents and photographs reproduced in this book. Richard Veazey, head of the Rasmuson Library's photography department, quickly and expertly provided digital images of the archival photographs and documents.

The online photo library at the National Oceanic and Atmospheric Administration (NOAA) is the source of the vintage illustrations of 19th century marine mammal harvest activities in the Bering Sea. Most of the etchings were created by H.W. Elliot, who was dispatched by the U.S. Commission of Fish and Fisheries (precursor to NOAA Fisheries) to the Bering Sea and other parts of the world on a mission to document U.S. fisheries in the late 1800s.

We used as many photos as we could find that were recorded in the Bering Sea and Aleutian Islands region. However, instead of omitting pictures of important species when we could not locate photos shot in the subject region, we chose to use photographs recorded elsewhere, most in other Alaska or North Pacific waters. Some photos of cetaceans were shot off the California coast, and the polar bears were photographed in northern Canada.

Harriman Expedition

In 1899, railroad magnate Edward H. Harriman organized a trip that took him and a cadre of scientists, artists, conservationists, and friends to the seas and coasts of Alaska and the Russian Far East. Among the passengers were conservationist John Muir, nature writer John Burroughs, and photographer Edward Curtis.

In 2001, the Clark Science Center of Smith College organized a trip that retraced the course of the Harriman Expedition. As in the original trip, the passenger list for the 2001 expedition included scientists, artists, and conservationists.

Alison Hammer, a physical scientist with the NOAA National Ocean Service, was one of the passengers. Hammer generously provided excellent photos she recorded on the trip. We are especially grateful for the images that depict people and places on the Bering Sea coast of Russia. An outstanding two-hour video about the two Harriman voyages is available from the Public Broadcasting System.

Expert advice

Many subject-matter experts provided information and reviewed the text. These people and other sources are listed in the Resources and Personal Communication sections at the back of the book. We gratefully acknowledge their interest in this project and sharing of knowledge.

The magicians

This book could not have been produced without the expert behind-the-scenes work of three stalwart and skilled ASG staff members. Sue Keller, editor and publications manager, proofread and helped edit the text, and compiled the index and resources section. Kathy Kurtenbach, publications coordinator, and Tatiana Piatanova, graphics manager, worked determinedly—and patiently—with the editors through what seemed like countless iterations to prepare the book for the printer.

Printing was coordinated by Warren Fraser of the University of Alaska Press and UAF Printing Services.

Just the facts

As with all ASG publications, we worked diligently to present factual information derived from credible sources and tapped knowledgable people to review the text. However, even experts sometimes disagree on presentation or interpretation of facts. If, during your voyage of discovery through this book, you uncover errors, please bring them to our attention.

NPMR and ASG/NOAA funding acknowledgments appear elsewhere in the front matter of this book.

The Bering Sea

INTRODUCTION

T he Bering Sea is America's backyard ocean. It is 885,000 square miles (2.3 million sq km) of the coldest, stormiest, bleakest ocean in the world. And this great sea also is one of the most biologically productive.

Tens of thousands of people who live on both its western and eastern shores derive their subsistence from the Bering Sea and its tributaries. Thousands more, from Nome to Seattle, Tokyo to Oslo, Providenya to Vladivostok, make their livelihoods from those waters in commercial fishing and processing.

Alaska supplies about half of the total U.S. fishery, and the majority of Alaska's contribution is from the Bering Sea and Aleutians. The Bering Sea harvest is about three percent of the entire world fish catch. The pollock fishery is the nation's largest and contributes $1.5 billion to the national economy.

The Bering Sea offers promise of wealth in other industries as well. Petroleum and gas prospects have been identified on both sides of the sea, and with advancing technology the sea bottom eventually may be opened to oil drilling. Marine transportation, focused on the Northwest Passage through Arctic Canada and the Northern Sea Route over the top of Russia, could turn the Bering Sea into a corridor for much of the world's shipping.

Tourism is growing, and while visitors remain few, the industry has the potential of transforming previously remote locations into playgrounds for

ALISSA CRANDALL ©

St. George is a town of about 200 people on St. George Island in the Pribilof Islands. The Pribilofs are about 160 miles northwest of Dutch Harbor.

Left—Natural sea arch at the Elephant Toes, Nunavachak Bay, Togiak National Wildlife Refuge.
FRED HIRSCHMANN ©

Walrus at Round Island.

In addition to its many other values, the Bering Sea is immensely important to the nation and the world as a biological repository of species large and small.

affluent and influential vacationers.

The Bering Sea sits in a position of great strategic military importance should disagreements again arise between East and West.

In addition to its many other values, the Bering Sea is immensely important to the nation and the world as a biological repository of species large and small. Many of them are found nowhere else in the world, and most of their populations are relatively undisturbed by human activities.

Biologists count up to 450 species of fish and invertebrates in the sea, and 50 species of seabirds on its surface and its shores. More than 40 percent of all breeding seabirds in the United States inhabit the Bering Sea region, which equates to some 25 million individual birds. The Bering Sea also is home to 25 species of marine mammals.

It also is valuable as a laboratory for the study of climate, circulation, sediment and nutrient transport, ice, and a myriad of other physical, chemical, and biological relationships that are little understood by scientists. It is a place where global climate change, human impacts, and other forces acting on the environment can be studied. The sea is the object of intense international scientific research, in part because many see it as an indicator of the health of the entire planet.

The Bering Sea is the object of equally intense wrangling over conservation and allocation of its resources. Precipitous declines in populations of some birds, mammals, fish, and invertebrates have galvanized activists to press for drastic measures to reverse what they believe to be mismanagement of the resources.

Girls share a productive arctic char fishing hole at Nome.

1. Fur seal pups take a snooze on Bogoslof Island. 2. Fishermen in Russia empty chum and coho salmon from their gillnet. 3. Murres tend their eggs on Bogoslof Island. 4. A sea otter relaxes with its sea star meal at Amchitka in the Aleutian Islands. 5. The seafloor at Amchitka Island displays a kaleidoscope of colorful corals, sponges, and other sea life.

Issues like the steep declines in populations of the Steller sea lion, northern fur seal, harbor seal, and sea otter in the Aleutians have scientists and conservationists worried about changes in the environment. Allegations of massive overfishing and concern over the millions of pounds of fish wasted by some components of the fishing industry have polarized public opinion and split coastal communities into adversarial camps.

Scientists have discovered evidence of toxic contaminants in the tissues of birds, mammals, fish, and invertebrates.

Causes of the documented increase in atmospheric and sea surface temperatures and decrease in the extent of seasonal ice coverage, accompanied by apparent decreases in primary productivity, are subjects of intense debate among scientists and policy makers. An important question is whether these phenomena are the result of human-caused global warming or are related to much longer-term cycles in the earth's temperature.

Beyond the realm of conflict, Alaska's Bering Sea coast is the backdrop of increasingly visible and focused efforts by people committed to promoting sustainable use of those resources and improving the economic standard of living for coastal residents. Evolving political consciousness, advancing technology, shifts in biological productivity, and rapidly changing world markets—especially for seafood products—have created new challenges and new opportunities for the people of that remote coast.

The icy dark waters of the Bering Sea conceal many secrets. This book is intended to reveal a few that have been exposed through two centuries of industrial exploitation, and new discoveries that are now coming to light as a result of intensified scientific inquiry.

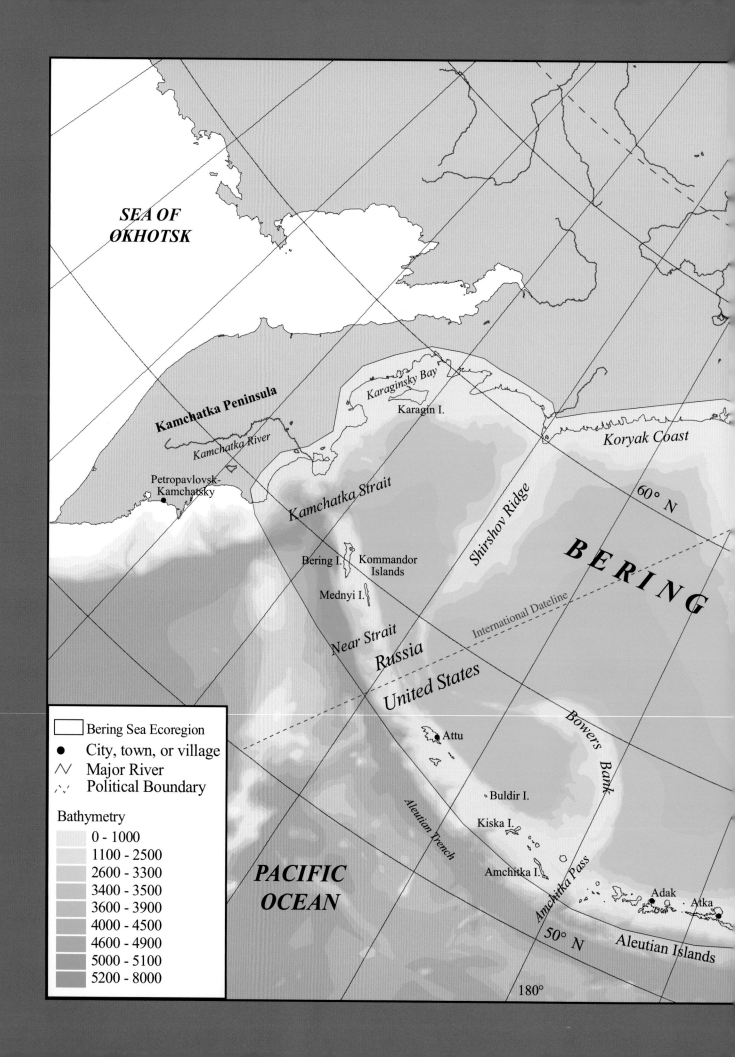

SEA OF
ØKHOTSK

Kamchatka Peninsula

Karaginsky Bay

Karagin I.

Kamchatka River

Koryak Coast

Petropavlovsk-
Kamchatsky

Kamchatka Strait

60° N

Shirshov Ridge

Bering I.
Kommandor
Islands

B E R I N G

Mednyi I.

International Dateline

Near Strait

Russia

United States

Bowers Bank

Attu

Buldir I.

Kiska I.

Aleutian Trench

Amchitka I.

Adak

Atka

Amchitka Pass

PACIFIC
OCEAN

50° N

Aleutian Islands

180°

Bering Sea Ecoregion

● City, town, or village

⋀ Major River
⋏⋅⋏ Political Boundary

Bathymetry

	0 - 1000
	1100 - 2500
	2600 - 3300
	3400 - 3500
	3600 - 3900
	4000 - 4500
	4600 - 4900
	5000 - 5100
	5200 - 8000

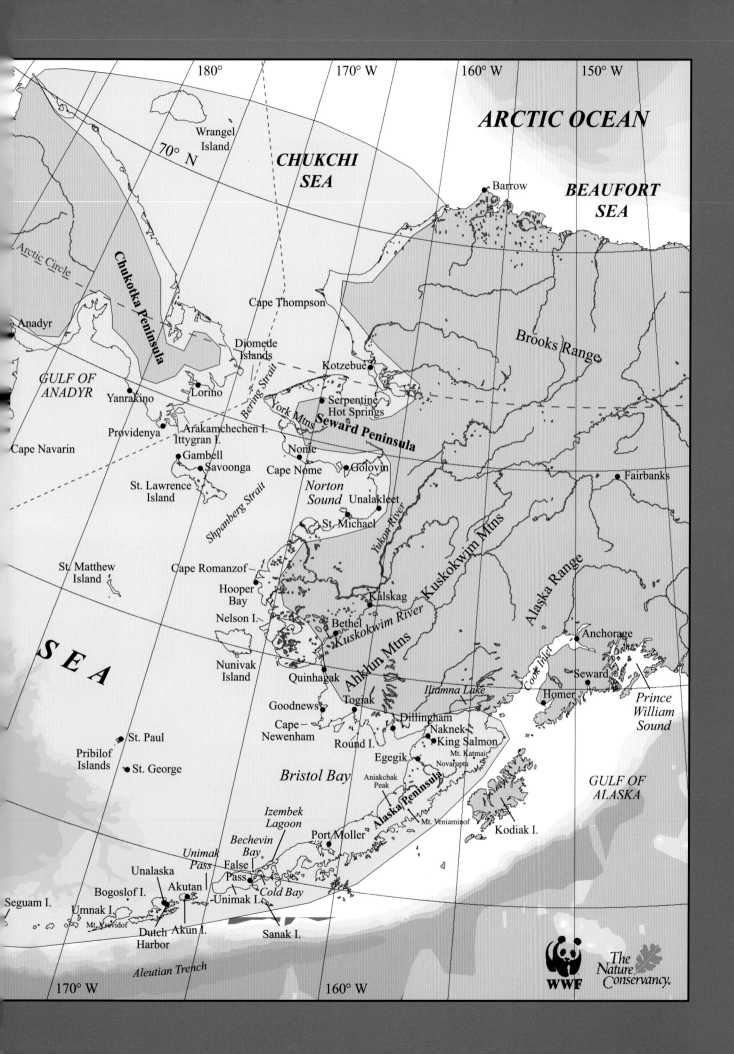

Global Context
CHAPTER ONE

Russian scientists dining with American colleagues at meetings concerning the Bering Sea may offer a toast that translates something like this: "To the Sea, which divides us and unites us."

Two of the world's greatest nations share an ocean boundary that is wide, harsh, and forbidding, yet bountiful for its aboriginal residents and more recent settlers, and ultimately finite in its ability to provide for humanity's demands for renewable resources.

The Bering Sea fills a huge marine basin, covering an area approximately as large as the continental United States west of the Mississippi. That basin is the most northerly extension of the North Pacific Ocean and it exchanges waters with the Gulf of Alaska through numerous passes in the Aleutian Islands, between the Aleutians and Russia's Kommandor Islands, and between the Kommandors and the Kamchatka Peninsula. It also is the Pacific's link to the Arctic Ocean via

PHOTO BY JAMES BARKER ©

Whale bones at Ittygran, Chukotka, rendered by Alaska artist Kes Woodward, during the 2001 retracing of the 1899 Harriman Expedition in the Bering Sea.

the Chukchi Sea, and feeds a steady flow of nutrient-rich water into the Chukchi through the 50-mile-wide (80 km) Bering Strait.

The Bering Strait, separating Alaska's Seward Peninsula from Russia's Chukotka Penin-

sula, is at the northern apex of this gigantic basin. The coasts of Kamchatka and Chukotka to the west, and western Alaska to the east, form the sides of this roughly triangular basin. Four large indentations—the Gulf of Anadyr and Karaginsky

Left— Photo of relief globe at UAF Geophysical Institute.

DAVID COCCIA ©

7

Vsevidof Volcano on Umnak Island in the Aleutians.

Formed by subduction of the Pacific Plate under the North American Plate, the region is the birthplace of much of the Pacific's earthquake activity.

Bay in Russia, and Bristol Bay and Norton Sound in Alaska, distort this three-sided outline. Maximum dimensions are 900 miles (1,500 km) north to south and 1,300 miles (2,000 km) east to west.

The southern margin of the triangle is the 1,300-mile arc of the Alaska Peninsula and the Aleutian Island–Kommandor Island chain. Comprising one of the most active parts of the Pacific's

Most notable in American waters are the Pribilofs, 220 miles (350 km) north of the Aleutians; St. Matthew, another 250 miles (400 km) to the northwest; St. Lawrence, which is some 200 miles (320 km) northeast of St. Matthew; and Nunivak, which lies just off the Yukon-Kuskokwim Delta. Several smaller islands are situated in Bristol Bay, Norton Sound, and in the Bering Strait. On the Russian

Bogoslof Island, one of some 200 islands in the Aleutian archipelago in the southern Bering Sea, was formed by volcanic forces. The tiny island is located about midway in the 1,000-mile-long Aleutian Island chain.

ring of fire, this string of 50-plus islands is studded with active as well as dormant volcanoes, some rising to as much as 5,000 feet (1,500 m) in elevation. Formed by subduction of the Pacific Plate under the North American Plate, it is the birthplace of much of the Pacific's earthquake activity, and in recent decades has spawned several destructive waves known as *tsunami*.

Other islands lie within the Bering Sea, a total of 150 in all.

side are Bering and Mednyi in the Kommandors group, Karagin and Verkhoturov in Karaginsky Bay adjacent to the Kamchatka Peninsula, Arakamchechen and Yttygran off Chukotka, and Big Diomede in the Bering Strait.

The most southerly point of the Bering Sea lies just above 51° north latitude, about the same as northern Vancouver Island, Quebec City, London, and Brussels. The Bering Strait lies at 66° north, just below the Arctic Circle, roughly parallel

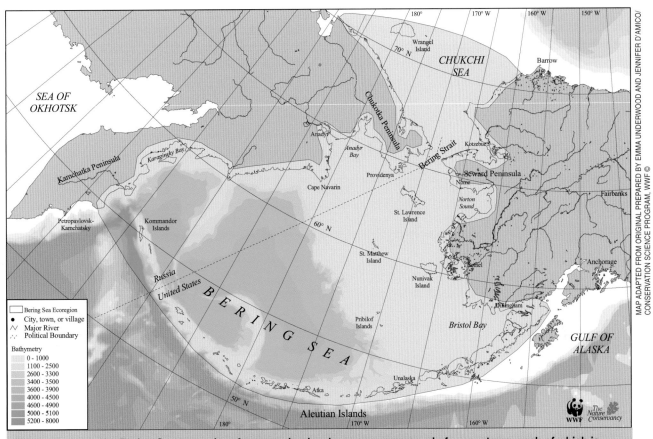

This map shows the Bering Sea ecoregion. An ecoregion is a large area composed of ecosystems, each of which is affected by plant and animal life and environmental conditions in one or more of the other ecosystems.

to northern Iceland and southern Lapland. The easternmost extent of Bristol Bay is at 157° west longitude, directly north of Molokai in the Hawaiian Islands. The lower Kamchatka coast is at about 162° east, which is due north of a point about midway between New Zealand and Australia.

The International Dateline splits the sea in two, with about two-thirds of it in today and the other third in tomorrow. If you fly two hours in a small plane from Nome to Providenya you are transported 23 hours into the future, and to return you get to re-live almost one full calendar day.

Coastline and rivers

While the Russian coast is mainly a rugged shore of cliffs and steep headlands, most of mainland Alaska's Bering Sea coast is low-lying tundra, gentle hills, and extensive tidal flats. Some places boast bold relief, like the Togiak area of Bristol Bay, the Askinuk Mountains at Cape Romanzof, parts of the Norton Sound coast, and the Cape York Mountains northwest of Nome. But great expanses of coastal plain are so low that they are not visible from a small boat traveling a safe distance off the beach. The

vast boggy region between the mouths of the Yukon and Kuskokwim rivers—known locally as the "Y-K Delta"—consists of 15,000 square miles (40,000 sq km) of lakes, ponds, rivers, and sloughs, none more than a few dozen feet (7 m) higher than the sea itself. Although tides at the mouth of the Yukon River are barely three feet (1 m), high tide raises the level of the river as far upstream as Head of Passes, some 50 miles from the ocean (80 km).

The Yukon River, with a delta of almost 2,500 square miles (6,500 sq km), is the second longest river in North

The Yukon, along with the Kuskokwim and scores of smaller rivers, contributes a huge volume of freshwater to the Bering Sea, as well as sediments and nutrients.

An aerial view shows the expansive low-lying coastal wetlands plain northeast of Bristol Bay.

America, after the Mississippi, and drains a region of Interior Alaska and northwest Canada about the size of Texas and Oklahoma combined. Its South Mouth alone, largest of the river's dozens of outlets, is eight miles wide (13 km). The Yukon, along with the Kuskokwim and scores of smaller rivers, contributes a huge volume of freshwater to the Bering Sea, as well as sediment and nutrients. The rivers provide spawning and rearing habitat for much of the Bering Sea fisheries wealth as well as rich nesting grounds for an abundance of waterfowl and shorebirds. Great rivers on the Russian side, like the Kamchatka and the Anadyr, also provide expanses of prime fish and wildlife habitat.

Continental shelf and sea ice

Two characteristics set the Bering Sea apart from other semi-enclosed, highly productive, international seas. One is the broad continental shelf that underlies the northeastern half of the sea. In many ways this shelf makes the Bering Sea what it is because the waters overlying the shelf are so

Pan ice forms on the Bering Sea. The Bering Sea's seasonal ice advance covers the greatest area of any arctic or subarctic ice advance.

shallow that currents and wind waves mix bottom sediments into the water column where sunlight penetrates, effectively fertilizing the sea with nutrients. This fertile ocean pasture boosts the photosynthesis that supports all ocean life.

The second characteristic is its seasonal ice covering. From about the end of November until early April the northern one-third to one-half is covered by a nearly impenetrable blanket of pack ice. The Bering Sea does not have icebergs, as there are no tidewater glaciers to calve them, but instead supports a thin but tightly packed layer of pan ice.

The ice forms in a southerly direction with the coming of winter, extending as much as 550 miles south (900 km). Due to a pool of warmer water in the deeper part of the sea beyond the continental shelf, the maximum extent of the ice is approximately that of the extent of the shelf itself. With the advent of spring, warming winds start melting the ice and the north flowing current carries the remnants back to the north, eventually through the Bering Strait and Chukchi Sea. The ice provides habitat for a range of mammals, fish, and birds, and also harbors and then releases algae that stimu-

late the sea's extraordinary biological productivity.

In recent years many adventurers have attempted to cross the ice on foot, skis, snowmachines, and even wheeled vehicles, all to no avail. A few Native people have crossed the Bering Strait in small boats, and a few commercial fishermen have taken their large steel vessels to Kamchatka from ports in the Aleutians. Otherwise, only air travel has succeeded in physically uniting people on the coasts of these two great nations that are divided by the Bering Sea.

Valuable resources

In a sense the Bering Sea is the center of a very large, very sparsely populated multicultural community. Its coastline is ringed by small, widely separated towns and villages. It is bridged by closely related cultures and languages—the Siberian Yupik of the Bering Strait region has family members on both sides. The material cultures (clothing, tools, homes) of aboriginal peoples on both sides are nearly identical, myth and legend are similar, and use and appreciation of natural resources practically a mirror image.

Those resources—salmon and herring, seal and walrus—provide subsistence for nearly 100,000 Native people on both sides, Aleut and Itel'men in the south, Koryak, Yupik and Chup'ik farther north, and Chukchi and Inupiaq by the

Walleye pollock from the Bering Sea.

By the early years of the twentieth century, stocks of nearly every marine mammal of commercial value had been depleted to the point of commercial non-viability.

Bering Strait. Even today, after more than two centuries of occupation by European invaders, Native peoples on the Bering Sea coast rely heavily on food from the sea and its shores. The high-power rifle and aluminum skiff have largely replaced the spear and the skin boat, and the nets are of nylon rather than plant fiber and sinew. But the mammals and fish obtained with these tools are still shared among family and community members and eaten in a fashion almost unchanged since pre-contact times.

Marine mammal exploitation

With the end of commercial walrus hunting on the Russian shore in the 1990s, marine mammals are essentially now all de-commercialized. True, mammal parts including walrus ivory and seal skins are still sold for cash, but only from animals ostensibly taken for subsistence.

The last real commercial hunt on the American side ended in the 1960s when the U.S. government ceased its subsidy of the Pribilof Islands fur seal slaughter. Seals are still taken in the islands but only to provide food and crafts materials for local people.

For more than a century fur seals had been harvested by the tens of thousands annually. The slaughter really got under way after Russians discovered the Pribilof Islands, where as many as two million fur seals once hauled out, mated, and pupped. Russian traders essentially enslaved Aleuts and relocated them from their homes in the Aleutians to the bleak Pribilofs, to do the butchery. Later, Japanese, Canadian, and American sealers continued the carnage. After the Fur Seal Treaty of 1966, only Pribilof residents remained in the business, supported by the U.S. government after the value of pelts dropped below the cost of production.

This is a rare skeleton of a Steller's sea cow, on display at the Museum of the Natural History of the Kommandor Islands in Nikolskoe, Russia. The sea cow is thought to have become extinct around 1768.

Russian hunters and traders also exploited the abundant and richly furred sea otter. As early as 1742 Russian hunters were taking otters, first on the Kamchatka side of the Bering Sea, then in the Aleutians, gradually advancing east and south. They established their capital at Sitka, mainly on the strength of sea otter stocks, and worked their way as far south as present-day Fort Ross and the Russian River in California. After the sea otters were depleted the Russian government had little use for Alaska and sold it to the United States in 1867.

Meanwhile, Yankee whalers had discovered productive grounds in the Bering and Chukchi seas. Over a period of decades they decimated the bowhead, sperm, fin, humpback, and gray whales in those waters. When the whales got scarce the whalers turned to walruses. By the early years of the twentieth century, stocks of nearly every marine mammal of commercial value had been depleted to the point of commercial non-viability.

Many marine mammal stocks, including walrus and gray whales, are making a comeback and recovering from years of heavy exploitation. Other Bering Sea mammals, including Steller sea lions, northern fur seals, and sea otters, have declined precipitously in the past three decades for unknown reasons. Only one marine mammal, the massive but docile Steller's sea cow, a relative of the manatee and dugong, has disappeared from the planet, and it was gone before commercial exploitation

THE FUR-SEAL INDUSTRY OF THE PRIBILOV ISLANDS, ALASKA.
Natives driving the "holluschickie"; the drive passing over the lagoon flats to the killing-ground, under the village hill, St. Paul's Island.
(Sect. v, vol. ii, p. 363.)
Drawing by H. W. Elliott.

Top—Native harvesters on the Pribilofs are depicted herding fur seals for slaughter in 1872. Bottom—The same herding technique still is used in a limited subsistence harvest that continues today.

even began. A single species of bird, the spectacled cormorant, met the same fate.

While sea otters, fur seals, and whales brought westerners to the Bering Sea, pollock, cod, salmon, and crab have kept them here.

Fish harvest

The fishery resources support thousands of people from Nome and Providenya to Seattle and Vladivostok, to Tokyo and Oslo. At any given time, thousands of people are riding the sea's tempestuous

A Naknek fisherman dresses a salmon.

The valuable fisheries of the Bering Sea are based on an extraordinarily productive marine ecosystem.

waters aboard trawlers, crabbers, longliners, and floating processors. Thousands more are at the sea's edge in processing plants and support facilities in places like Dutch Harbor, Akutan, and St. Paul, and in Vladivostok and Petropavlovsk-Kamchatsky on the Russian side. And that doesn't count dozens of small seasonal processing operations handling salmon and herring from several thousand small gillnetters, seiners, and skiffs catching the fish in bays and straits up one coast and down the other.

Bristol Bay alone supports a fleet of almost 3,000 small gillnetters and skiffs, and almost another thousand work the lower Kuskokwim and Yukon rivers and Norton Sound when fishing is open. Tiny villages like Egegik, Naknek, Clark's Point, Togiak, Quinhagak, Emmonak, and Unalakleet have seafood processing plants that buy product from local catchers and employ local workers.

These fishermen and processors, no matter how remote, are all part of the immense global food industry. A sockeye salmon plucked yesterday from the turbid waters of Bristol Bay may be featured tomorrow sliced, salted, and grilled as *aramaki* in an upscale Tokyo restaurant. The gangly king crab dumped on the deck of a pitching crabber plowing through a snowstorm on a wintry night north of Akutan will eventually become centerpiece of a family dinner in New York. Ersatz crab legs and white fish blocks destined for fast food restaurants

and supermarkets around the world are made from pollock scooped up by Bering Sea trawlers.

Participation in the global food industry makes these fisheries businesses and workers part of the global economy. They are affected by the price of oil in the Persian Gulf, the cost of capital on Wall Street, competition from producers in Russia and South America, and the whims of consumers around the world. Success or failure of their enterprise depends as much on an agreeable financial climate as on the stocks of fish and shellfish that they harvest. Owners of some of these vessels and processing plants are local people. But many are held by corporations based in Seattle, in northern Europe, and in Japan. What happens to fish in the Bering Sea affects people in many countries, and what happens in many countries in turn affects the marine resources of the Bering Sea.

Productive ecosystem

The valuable fisheries of the Bering Sea are based on an extraordinarily productive marine ecosystem. It may not seem logical that a cold, stormy northern sea, much of it covered by ice nearly half the year and lying under long nights of darkness for months at a time, could support such a productive marine food web. The land at that latitude is virtually worthless for farming, and wild

The big three Bering Sea fisheries are walleye pollock (top), sockeye salmon (right), and snow crab (bottom left). Many other species also are harvested from this fertile sea.

game is scarce. But high latitude waters in both the Northern and Southern Hemispheres sustain high levels of biological productivity. The abundance of cod off Iceland and Norway, and the once-great whale fisheries in Antarctic waters, attest to the ability of subpolar seas to support large populations of marine life.

Food web

All biological productivity starts with photosynthesis—plants capturing the sun's energy and converting carbon dioxide and water into sugars, which become living tissue. In the sea most photosynthesis is carried out by very small plant-like organisms called protists,

mostly microscopic single-celled algae such as diatoms, known as *phytoplankton*. The Bering Sea's long nights of winter are balanced by a six-month period each year when hours of sunlight exceed those of darkness. In the northern, most productive part of the sea, the sun's rays brighten the water column for more than 20

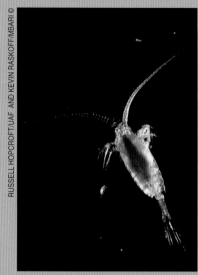

RUSSELL HOPCROFT/UAF AND KEVIN RASKOFF/MBARI ©

A copepod, a key component in the Bering Sea food web.

There is tremendous variability in the distribution and mixing of nutrients in the Bering Sea, and it is reflected in the variability of its overall productivity.

hours a day during June and July. In the long bright days of spring and early summer, phytoplankton organisms that have access to sufficient nutrients in the water suddenly and dramatically reproduce and increase their numbers by the thousands, creating what is known as plankton blooms.

The nutrients required by phytoplankton are composed mainly of nitrogen and mineral detritus dissolved in seawater or sediment suspended in it, plus organic materials like the decaying remains of dead plankton and various forms of animal life. Most nutrients in the sea, which are either contributed by rivers or transported into the region by currents, sink to the bottom. It is only when *mixing* stirs these nutrients into the water column, and brings them into the *euphotic* zone in the upper 30 feet or so (9 m) where there is a sufficient sunlight, that phytoplankton blooms can occur.

Phytoplankton are fed upon by *zooplankton*, mostly microscopic animals such as copepods that serve as the link to higher trophic level animals. A simplified model would be: (1) diatoms use sunlight and suspended inorganic nutrients; (2) they are fed upon by copepods; (3) euphausids (*krill*) eat the copepods and in turn are eaten by herring, sockeye salmon, and some baleen whales; (4) larger fish like pollock and cod eat the herring and young salmon, as do predatory mammals like seals and sea lions; (5) apex predators, including humans and toothed whales like orcas,

eat the seals and sea lions as well as herring and salmon. The actual system is much more complicated, which is why it is called a food web rather than a chain. It all starts with the lowly but incomprehensibly numerous single-celled algae.

In the Bering Sea a key component of the food web is the *benthic* (bottom dwelling) community of invertebrates, including polychaetes (worms), amphipods (marine "bugs"), bivalves (clams), gastropods (sea stars), crustaceans (shrimps and crabs), and numerous other animals. This complex community is composed of filter feeders (such as clams), detritus feeders (worms and some shrimps), and predators including sea stars and crabs. In the northern Bering Sea and into the Chukchi Sea, particularly in the biologically productive areas along the shelf break known as the *Green Belt,* a lot of the living biomass is in the benthos and provides the nutritional support for various bottom feeders, including the big populations of walruses and gray whales.

Access to nutrients

The foundation of the Bering Sea's productivity, given a limited and relatively fixed available amount of solar energy, is access to nutrients. Because of the abundance of rivers, the sea is reasonably well provided with sediments, made up of pulverized rock transported from the distant mountains to the sea. But river sediment is dumped more-or-less right at the river mouth

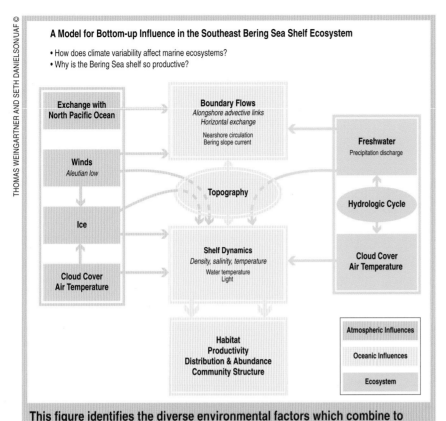

A Model for Bottom-up Influence in the Southeast Bering Sea Shelf Ecosystem

• How does climate variability affect marine ecosystems?
• Why is the Bering Sea shelf so productive?

Exchange with
North Pacific Ocean

Boundary Flows
Alongshore advective links
Horizontal exchange

Nearshore circulation
Bering slope current

Freshwater
Precipitation discharge

Winds
Aleutian low

Topography

Hydrologic Cycle

Ice

Shelf Dynamics
Density, salinity, temperature
Water temperature
Light

Cloud Cover
Air Temperature

Cloud Cover
Air Temperature

Habitat
Productivity
Distribution & Abundance
Community Structure

Atmospheric Influences

Oceanic Influences

Ecosystem

This figure identifies the diverse environmental factors which combine to make the Bering Sea an extraordinarily productive marine ecosystem.

and wouldn't do much for ocean productivity as a whole unless it were distributed by currents. The other source of nutrients is water entering the Bering Sea from the deep waters of the North Pacific through the Aleutian passes.

The key to sustained productivity, then, is effective transport and distribution of nutrients.

Various processes combine to accomplish this distribution, including currents within the sea, upwelling, tidal and wind wave mixing, and the effects of pressure ridges, temperature stratification (*thermoclines*) and salinity stratification (*haloclines*) in the water column. These processes work in different ways over the

continental shelf, the slope, and the deepwater basin that comprises the southwestern half of the Bering Sea.

Variable cycles

There is tremendous variability in the distribution and mixing of nutrients in the Bering Sea, and it is reflected in the variability of its overall productivity. Some is *interannual* (from one year to the next), such as the well-known *El Niño Southern Oscillation* phenomenon, and can be experienced in the form of sudden die-offs of particular species.

For example, in the summer of 1997 a persistent high pressure cell allowed sunlight to heat the surface layer of the sea while

lack of winds suppressed wave mixing, resulting in formation of a rigid thermocline across most of the Bering Sea. This had two dramatic effects: the warm surface layer supported a massive bloom of a *coccolithophore* diatom, normally scarce in the Bering Sea, which turned the water a milky aquamarine blue. The thermocline prevented essential nutrients from supporting a bloom of more nutritious phytoplankton and the zooplankton that feed on them, with the result that some seabirds, like shearwaters which feed on zooplankton, starved to death by the hundreds of thousands.

Other variability is in longer term cycles, fitting a pattern known as *decadal* (occurring over periods of ten years or more) *oscillation*, or as *regime shift*. Longer term oscillations may be expressed in long-term booms or downturns in production of commercial species like salmon, cod, and crab. Long-living mammals like whales, walruses, and sea lions show population shifts over periods of several decades, which may be the result of long-term variation in processes that move nutrients to phytoplankton photosynthesizers.

Thus the biological productivity of the Bering Sea, including the economic impact of commercial fisheries and the subsistence and aesthetic values for large mammals, fluctuates with atmospheric and oceanographic conditions, often outside the geographic confines of the sea itself.

Physical Environment
CHAPTER TWO

O ceanographic investigation of the Bering Sea began in earnest in the 1870s, and initially American vessels conducted most of the research cruises. In the 1920s Soviet scientists picked up the pace. The Soviets continued intensive research until the early 1990s when the breakup of the Soviet state deprived researchers of financial resources. Meanwhile, Japan, China, and other nations initiated their own scientific programs. Now most Bering Sea research is conducted by scientists from those four countries—United States, Russia, Japan, and China— separately and in joint expeditions.

Scientists have found a remarkable oceanic basin, the third largest semi-enclosed sea in the world. It has been formed and re-formed through millions of years by continental drift, volcanism, erosion and deposition, uplift and subduction, wind and wave action, and the repeated rising and lowering of sea level associated with

FRED HIRSCHMANN ©

Granite tors punctuate the landscape above Serpentine Hot Springs in the Bering Land Bridge National Preserve.

climate change and the advance and retreat of the world's ice caps.

Continental drift

The continents and seafloors comprise the surface layers of huge plates of hard rock that "float" on more fluid material closer to the earth's core. In terms of geologic time, these plates are constantly in motion, and as they bump into one another there is a great deal of grinding, pushing, folding, uplifting, and subsidence of plate surfaces. These processes are known as *plate tectonics*, and the plate tectonics theory explains many of the geological

Left—Sea ice on the Bering Sea.

Active fault zones are found in several areas, including along the Alaska Peninsula and the Aleutian Arc, with visible slumping, slides, and cliff collapse.

Okmok Mountain vents gases on Umnak Island in the Aleutians.

features we observe on the surface of the earth today.

The southern boundary of the Bering Sea is the line along which the northward moving Pacific Plate has been pushing against the North American Plate for hundreds of millions of years. The less dense North American plate has the upper hand in this collision and is gradually riding up onto the denser Pacific Plate. Subduction along part of the fault line continues at a rate of as much as three inches per year (7.6 cm). The result is that mountains like the Alaska Range to the north of the line of contact are ever-so-slowly being pushed skyward. To the south, where the Pacific Plate is subducting, the Aleutian Trench has become one of the deepest parts of the world's oceans.

Southwest Alaska is one of the most active seismic zones in the world, with nine earthquakes registering magnitude 8 or higher just in the last century. Two of the world's ten greatest recorded earthquakes in the last 100 years occurred in the Aleutians. Active fault zones are found in several areas, including along the Alaska Peninsula and the Aleutian Arc, with visible slumping, slides, and cliff collapse. Earthquakes have triggered numerous *tsunamis*, although those that have been destructive in Alaska were caused by quakes outside the Aleutians.

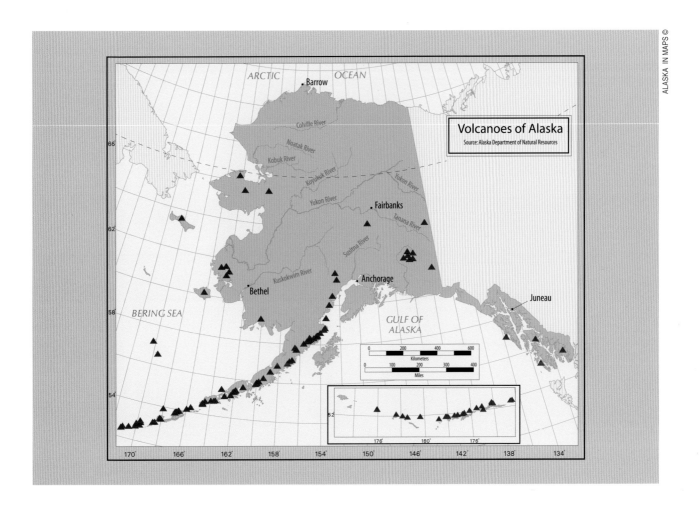

Volcanoes of Alaska
Source: Alaska Department of Natural Resources

Volcanism

A row of 40 historically active volcanoes marks the line of contact between the Pacific and North American plates. Volcanoes dot the landscape from upper Cook Inlet, down the spine of the Alaska Peninsula, and out to Kiska at the end of the Aleutian Chain. Still more volcanoes grace the Kommandor Islands and the Kamchatka Peninsula.

During an eruption, lava, cinders, and ash burst through the earth's surface at points of weakness in the globe's mantle, caused by the collision of the plates, and each volcano leaves a telltale conical peak. Many of

those eruptions have occurred below the surface of the sea, and only the tops of the mountains poke out of the water, making up many of the Aleutian Islands.

Because the lava of subduction zone volcanoes is less fluid than some other types of magma, it doesn't flow easily. This factor caused several volcanoes along the Aleutian Arc to develop plugs that backed up the flow of material. Pressure built to the point where it blew off the tops of the mountains, forming *calderas* like Aniakchak and Novarupta.

Many of those volcanoes remain active to this day, some

issuing constant puffs of steam, others occasionally blasting clouds of ash and dust that blanket thousands of square miles. Shishaldin Volcano on Unimak Island has erupted 25 times in the last two centuries. Several volcanoes on the Alaska Peninsula and in the Aleutians have erupted in recent years. The peninsula has one of the largest volcanoes in the world—Veniaminof—with a 30-mile-diameter base (50 km) and collapsed cone. The world's greatest eruption of the twentieth century occurred in 1912 when Novarupta exploded on the Alaska Peninsula.

The volcanic eruptions

U.S. GEOLOGICAL SURVEY ©

A volcano in
the Aleutians.

The arc of volcanic
mountains on the
Alaska Peninsula
and Aleutian Islands
cuts off the Bering
Sea basin from the
rest of the North
Pacific Ocean.

UAF ALASKA POLAR REGIONS DEPARTMENT ©

UAF ALASKA POLAR REGIONS DEPARTMENT ©

Top—Volcanic action creates Perry Island in the Aleutians. Bottom—U.S.
government workers pose on Bogoslof Island as Perry Island wells up from
the sea in 1907. Bogoslof Island was formed by similar volcanic action in 1796.

that formed the Aleutian Chain began as early as the late Cretaceous period 65 million years ago, and continue today. The creation of the Aleutian Ridge, even though it is partially permeated by dozens of shallow passes between the islands, separated the Bering Sea from the Pacific Ocean. The arc of volcanic mountains on the Alaska Peninsula and

Aleutian Islands cuts off the Bering Sea basin from the rest of the North Pacific Ocean.

The basin in the southwestern half of the Bering Sea has depths of 9,000-12,000 feet (3,000-4,000 m), and may have been an embayment of the North Pacific Ocean. It is nearly bisected by two ridges that are really submerged mountain ranges: the Shirshov Ridge

At 7,075 feet, Mt. Veniaminof on the Alaska Peninsula is one of the world's largest volcanoes.

which extends several hundred miles southeast from the Koryak coast of northern Kamchatka, and Bowers Bank which arcs north and west from the central Aleutians. Otherwise, the basin is a relatively flat floor of oceanic crust overlain by sedimentary materials, divided into three smaller basins: the Kommandor Basin is bordered by the Kamchatka mainland, the Kommandor Islands, and Shirshov Ridge. The Aleutian Basin lies between the Aleutian Islands and the continental shelf. And the much smaller Bowers Basin is nearly enclosed by Bowers Bank and the Aleutian Ridge.

Erosion and deposition

The floor of the Aleutian Basin is believed to consist of sedimentary deposits between one and five miles (2-9 km) thick overlying the Mesozoic oceanic crust, while the sediment layers in the Bowers and Kommandor basins are only one-half to two miles (1-3 km) deep.

The Bering Sea's continental shelf is made up of sediment deposited by the region's major rivers on top of a piece of the continental plate. Erosion of material from mountains on both the Alaskan and Russian sides contributed

sediment. The Yukon is believed to have deposited by far the greatest amount of sediment material, while the Kuskokwim, Kamchatka, and Anadyr rivers, along with numerous smaller rivers, also were important contributors.

During the late Miocene Epoch, between 5 million and 25 million years ago, uplift of the Alaska Range diverted into the Yukon River drainage watercourses that previously had flowed to the Pacific Ocean. This nearly doubled the volume of water and sediment the river contributed to the Bering Sea basin.

A hillside erodes in Western Alaska. Sediments eventually reach the sea, mostly via rivers and streams, and disperse near and far from their entry points.

The entire bottom on the continental shelf is fine or coarse grain sand, silt, clay, or gravel, and generally, the closer to shore the coarser the material.

The Yukon now deposits about 90 million tons of sediment into the sea annually, and the Kuskokwim another four million tons. Nevertheless, because the shelf is so broad and the transport to the north so great, the layer of sediment deposited on the southern shelf is only a few dozen feet thick (8 m), and on the northern shelf it is even less. These deposits have been made since the shelf was most recently submerged at the end of the last ice age 13,000 years ago.

Sedimentary deposition probably began during the early Tertiary Period, about 60 million years ago, at a time when the sea level was several hundred feet lower than it is now. The shelf started out as a broad alluvial (river deposited) plain. But during the Miocene Epoch of the later Tertiary sea level gradually rose.

For a period around ten million years ago the southern part of the basin was a sea as now. But the continental shelf was two broad plains consisting of portions of the Asian and North American blocks, gradually moving toward one another. The plain was divided by a wide, meandering channel, its waters flowing north and connecting that sea with the Arctic Ocean.

Shelf submerged

After rising waters submerged the continental shelf, sediment from the Yukon River was carried north through the Bering Strait by marine currents and deposited on the shelf of the Chukchi Sea, a process that continues today.

Other sediment is distributed over the shelf by the action of currents and by other forces such as wind and ice. That sediment is from the Kuskokwim, Kamchatka, Anadyr, and other rivers; from coastal erosion, especially along the Alaska coast; and also from volcanic activity. Silt and clay, and even pebbles, can be transported hundreds of miles frozen inside pan ice.

The fine particles are carried the farthest from shore by currents and are continuing to build the shelf outward from shore. Suspended sediments also are transported into the Bering Sea by the Alaska Coastal Current originating

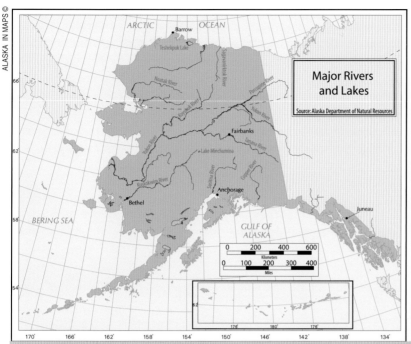

Major Rivers
and Lakes

Source: Alaska Department of Natural Resources

While major rivers including the Yukon and Kuskokwim contribute countless tons of sediment and freshwater to the Bering Sea each day, thousands of other small, unnamed streams like this one in the Aleutians also contribute to oceanic sediment deposition.

in the Gulf of Alaska.

The entire bottom on the continental shelf is fine or coarse grain sand, silt, clay, or gravel, and generally, the closer to shore the coarser the material. *Biogenic* materials, especially the shells of dead diatoms, comprise a significant component of the fine suspended sediments that settle out to cover the bottom, especially in the deep basins.

Evidence suggests that about five million years ago the channel bisecting the plain may have been blocked briefly, leaving a narrow land bridge between the Asian continent and Alaska. This was not, however, the *Bering Land Bridge* that emerged several million years later and allowed passage of many species of animals and plants, including

humans, to reach North America. The channel appears to have been reestablished during the Pliocene Epoch about three million years ago, and gradually widened to submerge the entire continental shelf and to give the Bering Sea its present configuration.

Glaciers

In the last couple of million years—the Pleistocene Epoch—the continental shelf has had numerous episodes of glacial advance and retreat, periods of lower and higher sea levels, and river sediment deposition. Glaciers have pushed as much as 100 miles (160 km) into the sea basin from the Russian side almost to St. Lawrence Island, and left moraine deposits in the form of gravel bars to the north

of the island. Glaciers also extended from the Alaska mainland well into Bristol Bay. The familiar contour of the Bering Sea's coast is not permanent but rather the present snapshot-in-time outline of a sea that continues to evolve.

The continental shelf today

The continental shelf is the Bering Sea's signature characteristic. Comprising more than 400,000 square miles (1,000,000 sq km) of smooth, almost featureless seafloor, it underlies waters no deeper than 300 feet (100 m) and has a gradient of less than half of one degree or only about 15 inches per mile, reputed to be the gentlest in the world.

An area the size of California has a depth of less than

Artist's rendering of the Bering Sea.

A small boat running miles offshore of the Bering Sea's Alaskan coast may be in water of a depth less than the boat's own length.

50 feet (17 m). A small boat running miles offshore of the Bering Sea's Alaskan coast may be in water of a depth less than the boat's own length.

The outer edge of the shelf, bisecting the sea roughly in a northwest-southeast direction, is the continental margin or continental slope. The gradient is much steeper than on the shelf. The margin begins at the 100 fathom (600 foot, 200 meter) contour, and within a short distance drops off to the abyssal depths. The slope isn't a straight diagonal line but rather it is a meandering margin and is incised by seven large submarine canyons.

Although 80 percent of the shelf underlies the eastern half of the Bering Sea, it doesn't dead-end at Russia's Koryak coast. Instead it continues as a narrower band of shallow water 50 to 100 miles wide (80-160 km) all the way down the eastern side of Kamchatka, and includes Karaginsky Bay.

Natural resources on the shelf

The distribution of sedimentary materials that formed the continental shelf, laid down over millions of years, has economic implications for the present-day nations that border the sea. The greater part of the continental shelf lies on the U.S. side of the international boundary. This conveys most of the productive marine habitat to the U.S. EEZ (Exclusive Economic Zone, or "200-mile limit"), making most of the valuable finfish and shellfish stocks available to American fishermen.

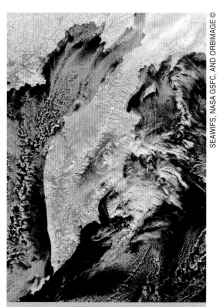

This is a satellite view of the Kamchatka Peninsula in Russia. The Sea of Okhotsk is to the left, the Bering Sea to the right.

It also provides American access to mineral deposits (gold, tin, platinum, mercury), natural gas, and oil reserves which may lie beneath the waves, allowing the potential advantage of working in water only hundreds of feet deep instead of ten thousand. More information is in Chapter 5.

The basin and continental shelf

Six physiographic zones characterize the Bering Sea: The Bering Sea Basin, the continental slope, the continental shelf, the islands, the adjacent North Pacific Ocean, and the coastal topography of its eastern and western shores. Each of these zones exerts an influence on water circulation patterns within the sea, which in turn influence primary biological productivity, the basis for

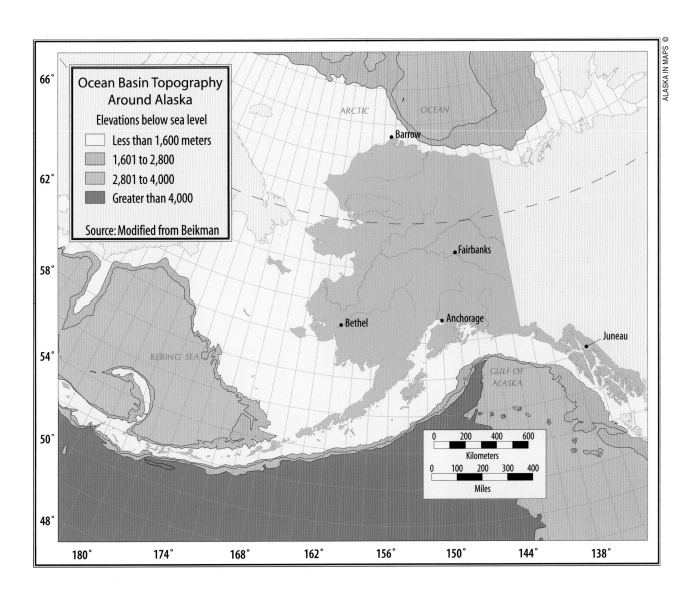

Ocean Basin Topography Around Alaska

Elevations below sea level

- Less than 1,600 meters
- 1,601 to 2,800
- 2,801 to 4,000
- Greater than 4,000

Source: Modified from Beikman

production and distribution of all living sea resources including upper trophic level mammals, fishes, and birds.

Abyssal basin

The abyssal basin, whose nearly flat bottom slopes downward very gradually from all sides toward the center, lies between 9,000 and 12,000 feet below sea level (3,000-4,000 m). Seafloor *bathymetric* charts show this basin ringed by a dense band of contour lines to the east and northeast (the slope edge of the broad continental shelf), to the west and northwest (the abrupt edge of the narrow shelf off the Kamchatka coast), and especially to the south.

The floor of the basin is believed to consist of Mesozoic oceanic crust rock overlain by sediment 1.5-5.5 miles thick (2.5-9 km). The rugged submarine terrains of the Aleutian Trench (just south of the Bering Sea proper), Aleutian shelf, Shirshov Ridge, and Bowers Bank constitute a dramatic contrast to the nearly flat bottom of the basin.

Shelf domains

The slope, the shelf edge, and the shelf itself are the nursery and rearing grounds for many of the finfish and shellfish stocks that support the sea's fishery wealth. Biological productivity is not evenly distributed across this expansive shelf, however.

The sea over the shelf is divided into several broad areas, called *domains*, which are separated from one another by *fronts* or lines of greatly differing seawater properties

Legendary monolith, Togiak National Wildlife Refuge.

FRED HIRSCHMANN ©

Several key locations along the shelf break, collectively known as the Green Belt, support much of the Bering Sea's biological productivity.

like salinity and temperature. The fronts have increased vertical mixing and tend to be very productive compared to the waters on either side. The *coastal domain* consists of waters less than 150 feet deep (50 m). The water here tends to be mixed from top to bottom during the ice-free season.

The *middle domain* is the broad band covering depths of 150-300 feet (50-100 m). The water is too deep for complete vertical mixing. The bottom water is mixed by tidal action and the surface water by the wind, so there is a two-layer water column, with a layer of warmer water at the top. This domain is less productive in the summer because bottom nutrients can't reach the growing phytoplankton near the surface. The outer edge of the middle domain has a shelf break front which separates coastal waters from the basin.

The *outer domain* may have three or more layers, essentially unmixed with one another and exhibiting different temperatures and currents.

Compared with the abyssal floor, the shelf has more widely spaced *isobaths* (lines connecting points of equal depth, similar to contour lines on a topographic map). Most isobaths parallel the western Alaska coast, indicating a very gradual, progressive increase in depth to about 600 feet (200 m) at the shelf break. The isobaths are more evenly spaced for the first couple of hundred miles from the coastline, but bunch up around Nunivak, St. Matthew, St. Lawrence, and the Pribilof Islands, indicating

irregularities in the submarine terrain. These irregularities in the bottom profile influence current flow and nutrient delivery that stimulate or retard biological productivity.

Green Belt at the shelf break

Several key locations along the shelf break, collectively known as the *Green Belt,* support much of the Bering Sea's biological productivity. Currents, especially the Bering Slope Current, deliver exceptional concentrations of nutrients at these locations, causing them to be biological hot spots. Tidal transport is the mechanism that contributes this nutrient supply to the shelf.

Circulation features like eddies, and *physiographic features* like canyons that lie in the continental slope cause nutrients to concentrate in certain locations.

Tidal mixing is a major factor in cross-shelf exchange. Other regions of the shelf, particularly along western Norton Sound and elsewhere in the sediment plume of the Yukon and Kuskokwim rivers, are relative "deserts," at least on the ocean floor.

The Gulf of Anadyr is a basin-within-a-basin, sloping gently from all sides toward its shallow center. Despite its high latitude and lengthy period of ice cover, the Gulf of Anadyr is one of the most productive regions in the sea. It is fed nutrients from the deep basin, the mighty Anadyr River, and the Bering Slope Current.

To the east of the Gulf of

A reindeer skull and antlers slowly decompose on the Seward Peninsula tundra, returning nutrients to the soil.

Anadyr, the area between St. Lawrence Island and the Bering Strait also has more irregular bottom topography than most of the continental shelf, and is one of the most productive of the sea's Green Belt regions.

Coastal topography

Although in our lifetimes we'll never see the underwater canyons and plains of the Bering Sea bottom, we know something about them from extensive echo soundings made by research vessels, and by various trawls, dredges, scooping, grabbing, and core drilling devices deployed to gather information.

But above water, just on the other side of that thin and fragile boundary known as the shoreline, a great deal more of the basin's physiography is observable.

Seward Peninsula

The uplands of the Seward Peninsula, on the Alaska side of the Bering Strait, feature broad, low mountains of up to 4,600 feet (1,500 m) and V-shaped valleys. The bedrock is *metamorphosed* (hardened by heat, pressure, or stress) mica, schist, marble, and other rocks of sedimentary and volcanic origin. Soils are wet and poorly drained gravel material, and vegetation is moist tundra at lower elevations and sparse mixed spruce and hardwoods along the rivers and in the hills.

Ground cover on the mountain slopes is alpine heath tundra. Reindeer were introduced in the late nineteenth century and herds are still kept by local Native people.

Yukon-Kuskokwim Delta

Farther south, the Yukon-Kuskokwim Delta is even flatter and wetter. A detailed topographical map of the region reveals thousand of lakes and ponds connected by thousands of miles of sloughs, channels, and rivers. Sedimentary soils locked in *permafrost* (permanently frozen ground) also form an impermeable basement to this botanically carpeted landscape. Nearly 80 percent of the surface is wetlands, and like the region

Wild irises in
Western Alaska.

Extensive tide
flats, some of them
several miles wide,
characterize the
mouths of major
rivers, the same
rivers that support
millions of spawn-
ing sockeye salmon
each summer.

1. Coastal flats on Bristol Bay. 2. Grass wetlands on the Yukon-Kuskokwim Delta. 3 & 4. Hillside tundra on the Seward Peninsula (3 with reindeer). 5. Landscape in Western Alaska. 6. Striated rock formation on the Bristol Bay coast.

to the north, the average annual temperature is below freezing.

Bristol Bay area

The Kuskokwim Mountains separate the watershed of the Kuskokwim River from that of Bristol Bay. The Ahklun Mountains comprise the westernmost extent of that range, and they terminate at Cape Newenham, thereby separating the Yukon-Kuskokwim Delta from the Bristol Bay lowlands, just as Cape Newenham separates the Kuskokwim from Bristol Bay.

Underlying the Bristol Bay lowlands is gravelly glacial till, outwash, and moraine materials from the rocks of the nearby mountains, covered by layers of silt and peat.

Tundra dominates the lowland, with shrubby birch, alder, and willow. Spruce and mixed hardwoods grow along the streams and on the mountainsides.

The northwestern side of the Bristol Bay region is generally hilly, whereas the southern and eastern sides comprise a broad lowland plain backed by the mountains of the Alaska Peninsula.

Extensive tide flats, some of them several miles wide, characterize the mouths of major rivers, the rivers that support millions of spawning sockeye salmon each summer.

Alaska Peninsula

The coastal plain of the Alaska Peninsula occupies the northern (Bristol Bay) side as far west as the extensive tidal inlet known as Izembek Lagoon, which contains one of the world's

Brown bears inhabit the Bering Sea coastal area of Western Alaska, with a density of something less than 13 bears per 1,000 square miles. Pictured here is a brown bear and cubs on the shore of Lake Naknek near Bristol Bay.

largest eelgrass beds.

The mountains were heavily glaciated during the Pleistocene, between 10,000 and 1.8 million years ago. They reach as high as 8,250 feet (2,750 m), and are composed of folded sedimentary rocks with intrusions of volcanic materials, with some calderas.

Most soils are glacial deposits and volcanic ash. Vegetative cover is alpine heath meadows, with willow and alders in low areas and along streams, and barren patches at higher elevations. Although wetlands cover a lower percentage of the Alaska Peninsula landscape than elsewhere on the Bering Sea coast due to soil type and steep relief, precipitation is actually much higher there. The average annual temperature is above freezing.

Aleutian Islands

To the west, beyond Bechevin Bay and False Pass at the very end of the peninsula, the topography turns to Aleutian, with steep hills, shoreside cliffs, and volcanic peaks on the north side of the islands to heights of as much as 6,230 feet (2,080 m). Other mountains are parts of tilted fault blocks. Some islands have terraces formed by wave action as much as 600 feet (200 m) above the current sea level. Many have lakes in basins carved out by glaciers. Soils are volcanic ash or *scoria* (cinder) materials. Vegetation is alpine heath meadows and lichen communities, with moist tundra at some lower elevation sites. Precipitation is a little greater and the average temperature is slightly higher than on the Alaska Peninsula.

An Aleutian bog.

Waters from the North Pacific filter through the Aleutian Islands, bringing with them nutrients that feed the plankton and support the Bering Sea's abundant sea life.

The jagged appearance of these tectonically generated Aleutian islands not yet worn down by erosion attest to their relatively young geologic age.

Physical Environment

Currents

Source of Bering Sea waters

Waters from the North Pacific filter through the Aleutian Islands, bringing with them nutrients that feed the plankton and support the Bering Sea's abundant sea life.

These waters arrive at the Aleutian chain from a couple of sources. Surface waters of the Alaska Coastal Current blend with the Alaskan Stream and enter the Bering Sea through the eastern Aleutian passes. Other waters come to this remote part of the world via one of the earth's most remarkable mechanisms, a deepwater ocean "conveyor belt" that revolves around the entire Western Hemisphere, linking waters of the Atlantic with Pacific, Arctic with Antarctic.

In the far North Atlantic, between Greenland and Northern Norway, the seawater is exposed to some of the most severely cold atmospheric temperatures on the planet. The water becomes very cold and more salty and therefore dense, so it sinks to lower depths in the Atlantic as it slowly moves southward.

The cold water of this slow-moving "river" works its way down the mid-Atlantic, along the east coast of South America, and eventually to Cape Horn at the continent's southern tip, only a few hundred miles from the glaciers of Antarctica. There it turns right and flows north again, through the abyssal depth of the Pacific Ocean and eventually to the Gulf of Alaska. Some of this water, following the contours of the sea bottom, is pushed to the surface and turns to flow south again. But some of it rises up from the Aleutian Trench to flow over the Aleutian Ridge and through the passes into the Bering Sea. This journey takes thousands of years.

Net northward transport

Once inside the Bering Sea, the water divides into dozens of currents, gyres, and eddies, with water moving in complicated patterns. Some of the water entering the western passes just whirls around and joins the Kamchatka Current to exit again via the Kamchatka Strait. Some of it spins around in small eddies just north of the Aleutian Islands, or in greater gyres in the abyssal depths of the Bering Sea basin. One major current flows in a northeasterly direction up the north side of the islands and the Alaska Peninsula and then splits; one branch flows northwest along the shelf edge; and the other rises up and spreads out over the shelf, dividing into several lesser currents while flowing north.

Although a great deal of water enters the Bering Sea through the passes, and more is added by the many rivers along its shores and by precipitation, most of it exits back into the Pacific. Only about five percent of all the water entering from the south exits through the Bering Strait to the north, but this small percentage results in general northward transport.

This all works because the Pacific Ocean is ever so slightly (18 inches, 45 cm) higher than the Atlantic due to differences in atmospheric pressure. The water flows downhill from the North Pacific Ocean through the Bering Sea and Arctic Ocean, back to the Atlantic Ocean.

Bering Slope Current

The big river of seawater that travels in a northwestward direction along the continental slope is known to oceanographers as the Bering Slope Current. Just as it is about to reach the Russian coast south of Cape Navarin it splits in two, with part of it going southwest to become the Kamchatka Current. The other part flows north, through the Gulf of Anadyr, past St. Lawrence Island, and eventually through the western channel of the Bering Strait.

The Bering Slope Current water is of high salinity but is diluted by Anadyr water. After passing through the Anadyr Strait it mixes with warmer and less salty Alaska Coastal Water and Norton Sound Water. The waters of the currents have traveled north over the continental shelf off the western Alaska coast, through the Shpanberg Strait between St. Lawrence and the Yukon Delta, and through the eastern channel of the Bering Strait.

The coastal water, containing sediments from the Yukon and Kuskokwim rivers, is slow moving and nutrient depleted. But the Bering Slope Current

Shoreline on St. Paul Island in the Pribilofs.

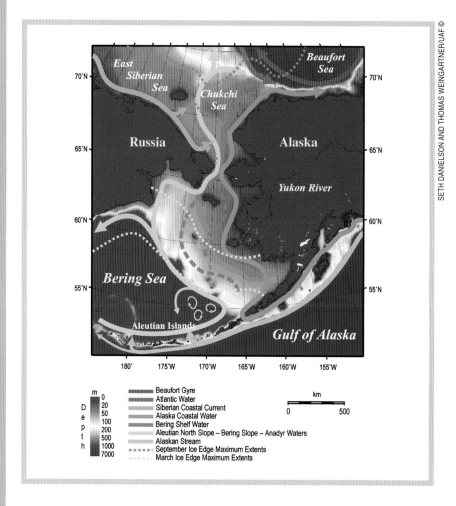

D e p t h	m
	0
	20
	50
	100
	200
	500
	1000
	7000

Beaufort Gyre
Atlantic Water
Siberian Coastal Current
Alaska Coastal Water
Bering Shelf Water
Aleutian North Slope – Bering Slope – Anadyr Waters
Alaskan Stream
September Ice Edge Maximum Extents
March Ice Edge Maximum Extents

km

0   500

One of the most
important areas
is the "deposition
center" north of
St. Lawrence Island,
which supports one
of the richest com-
munities of benthic
creatures in the
world.

water is nutrient rich and where it flows up onto the shelf it contributes to bands of high primary productivity, making up the *Green Belt*. One of the most important areas is the "deposition center" north of St. Lawrence Island, which supports one of the richest communities of *benthic* (bottom-dwelling) creatures in the world.

Alaskan Stream

While scientists have done extensive data collection and computer modeling of the Bering Sea's surface currents, they have less information about the flow of water at greater depths. Some data

suggests that most of the transport is in the upper 500 meters of the water column. It appears that water in the abyssal basin flows slowly, in kind of a giant counterclockwise gyre, deflected by the Bowers Ridge and the Shirshov Ridge. The Bering Sea is fed mainly by waters from the North Pacific–Gulf of Alaska, including a surface flow called the Alaskan Stream. These waters filter through the 14 major passes between the islands of the Aleutian-Kommandor chain. Rivers on both sides contribute waters as well.

Since there are no deepwater passes (more than 600 feet,

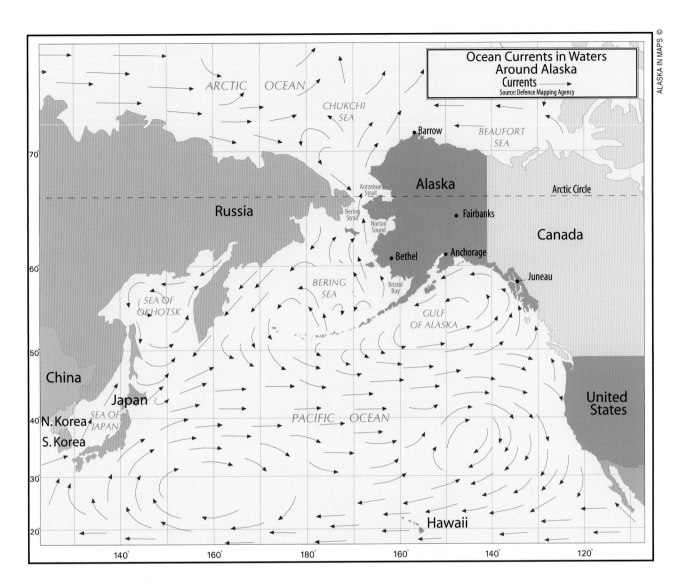

Ocean Currents in Waters Around Alaska
Currents ⟶
Source: Defence Mapping Agency

200 m) in the eastern Aleutians, most of the water enters through Near Strait (at the international boundary between Attu and the Kommandors), Amchitka Pass, and other western passes.

Alaska Coastal Current

Water from the Alaska Coastal Current (which flows along the coast from Southeast Alaska to the Aleutians) also enters the Bering Sea through Unimak Pass, the first significant

opening after the end of the Alaska Peninsula. From there it flows straight onto the shelf and transports much of the nutrient supply to the shelf area.

In response to tides, water flows in both directions and much that enters the abyssal basin through Near Strait exits again via Kamchatka Strait between the Kommandors and Kamchatka. Some of the Aleutian passes have currents running in both directions, and some have net outflows of water. A geographic/hydro-

graphic profile of the Aleutian Arc is a sawtooth pattern of sharp peaks and deep V-shaped underwater valleys of different depths, and waters ebb and flow through those passes in identifiable patterns.

Once inside the basin, currents distribute water in several directions. Below about 600 feet (200 m) Pacific water dominates and has very slow motion toward the north. In the upper layer is a complex circulation pattern, generally counter-clockwise.

Tideline at Cape Dezhnev.

Tides are a major force in cross-shelf transport of water and nutrients, and their effect is intensified around islands, bringing nutrient-rich water and plankton to provide a productive environment.

Aleutian North Slope Current

The undersea topography of the Aleutian chain imparts eddies and spins to some currents. The Aleutian North Slope Current flows eastward from the central Aleutians toward the Alaska mainland and the continental shelf. A swift current, it travels at one-fifth to one-third of a knot, considerably faster than currents in the deep basin. (A knot is one nautical mile per hour, about 1.15 mph, or about 0.51 meters per second). The steep rise of the continental slope directs much of the water into a northwest-flowing Bering Slope Current, and at the same time creates an upwelling that brings water up onto the shelf.

Tides

In the Bering Sea, as in other oceans, tides have a significant influence on water movement. In fact, about 90 percent of the *kinetic energy* (the energy involved in the motion of matter) over the Bering Sea shelf derives from tidal action. Barely perceptible at sea, tides have a great deal of effect in shallows and along the shore-lines. Tides are also a force in nutrient and organism transport, and mixing. On the continental shelf, Bering Sea tides are believed to have sufficient energy to mix (stir up sediments and nutrients) the water in the lower 130 feet (40 m) of the water column.

Tidal transport can be very

S E A   S C I E N C E

The great mixing bowl

Scientists call the northeast Bering Sea, where deep ocean water meets the continental shelf, a "Green Belt" because of its high springtime plankton production. Nutrients that fuel the Bering Sea's diverse ecosystem well-up here from the deep ocean.

NMPR researchers studied the mechanisms that allow this to happen. They found that the Bering Slope Current creates eddies as it flows northwestward along the continental shelf. These enormous eddies occur as closed loops dozens of miles in diameter and as much as 1,800 feet deep or more. Most, but not all, of these so-called "meso-scale eddies" spin counter-clockwise.

But any way they spin, moving at the rate of about 8 centimeters per second, these eddies gather nutrients from the deep ocean and spin them up onto the continental shelf, providing food for phytoplankton and zooplankton. The eddies also transport newly hatched fish and crab larvae.

Scientists say in spring when these eddies are strong along the shelf and there are elevated chlorophyll concentrations, plankton production tends to be high—which is a good thing.

Low tide exposes a coarse sand and gravel intertidal zone at Nome.

important to local ocean productivity. For example, tidal currents flowing around the Pribilof Islands trap nutrients and plankton close to the islands, making those nearshore waters exceptionally productive.

Causes of tides

Tidal patterns in the Bering Sea are complex, and are influenced by *tidal waves* from the Pacific Ocean, and to a very small extent from the Arctic. A tidal wave is the surge of water that flows into a part of the sea, raising or lowering its surface level, in response to the gravitational pull of the sun and moon. It is a very large-scale phenomenon. Sometimes the term "tidal wave" is incorrectly used for *tsunami*, which is an abrupt wave caused by an earthquake.

Tides in most of the Bering Sea are driven by the tidal wave of the Pacific Ocean, coming through the Aleutian passes. The Arctic tidal wave, averaging only about four inches (10 cm), has less influence. The surge of Pacific water flows over the Aleutian Shelf, into the Aleutian Basin, and up onto the continental shelf. As it moves northward it divides into several branches, each moving at different speeds due to varied underwater topography. As these waves approach the coastline, they produce tides of different amplitudes.

The nature of tides

Tides in most of the world are *semi-diurnal*, meaning that there are two complete cycles of high and low water each day. Most parts of the Bering Sea coast also have semi-diurnal tides, but in a few locations the tides are diurnal (a single cycle a day), or they have a modified pattern of one and a half tides a day. Parts of the eastern and western Aleutians, the coast of the Yukon Delta and Norton Sound, and part of the Kamchatka coast have diurnal tides. Some semi-enclosed embayments, such as Nanvak Bay near Cape Newenham, also have diurnal tides.

Tides are often described by their *amplitude* (or *range*), and *phase*. Range is the difference in the sea surface height between high tide and the next low tide; amplitude is half that, or the difference between sea level at mid-tide and high tide. Tidal phases, like phases of the moon, describe the monthly and annual cycle.

There is a great deal of variation in tidal range and current direction and speed at different locations in the world. Parts of the Alaska coast of the Bering Sea have some of the biggest variations in height and some of the swiftest tidal currents. Tides at St. Lawrence Island and in the Bering Strait are only about 7.5-12 feet (2.5-4 m), and in the Aleutians only five to six feet (1.5-2 m). Average daily range in Bristol Bay is 12-18 feet (4-6 m) and the extreme range during *spring tides* (having maximum range due to the alignment of sun and moon) is as much as 22 feet (7 m) in some locations.

Tidal currents over the shelf average about four-tenths of a knot, but in some of the Aleutian Islands passes, and in the upper reaches of some Bristol Bay estuaries, they flow

Broken cloud cover over the Aleutians.

Storm waves 40 feet high (about the height of a four story building) are common in the Bering Sea and can rise as high as 52 feet.

This satellite image shows a huge swirling cloud mass that indicates a low pressure system over the Bering Sea. The small turquoise area is part of a plankton bloom.

at more than two knots.

Tides are a major force in cross-shelf transport of water and nutrients, and their effect is intensified around islands, bringing nutrient-rich water and plankton to provide a productive environment.

Wind, waves, and storm surges

The Bering Sea is famous for storms that produce big waves. Most waves are wind-driven, although their height and shape are influenced by currents,

tides, bottom configuration, and island or coastal topography. Sharp atmospheric pressure differentials are common in the Aleutians and southern Bering Sea, and these pressure ridges create strong winds, especially in fall and winter. The biggest waves usually form over open, deep water, but as they enter shallower waters they become steep and often more dangerous to vessels. The northern Bering Sea is ice-covered half the year so wave heights are much smaller there in winter despite strong winds.

Russian scientists calculate that in the southern Bering Sea wind waves exceed 20 feet in height (6 m) about eight percent of the time in the winter, and 1.5 percent in the summer. Storm waves 40 feet high (about the height of a four story building) are common in the Bering Sea and can rise as high as 52 feet. During the summer, wind waves are six feet high (2 m) for 40-60 percent of the time.

Swells are waves with a *long period* (spaced hundreds of yards apart), generated by winds sometimes hundreds or even thousands of miles away. The Aleutian Islands break up the big Pacific swells, but swells as much as 24 feet high (8 m) can build within the Bering Sea.

Storm surges are infrequent, sudden localized areas of raised sea level, most often observed at coastal locations, caused by onshore winds in a storm. They usually occur during fall and winter. Combined with high tides and areas of low atmospheric pressure, storm surges can raise the water level enough to flood low-lying coastal villages and back up rivers. Storm surges of 4.5 feet (1.5 m) have been recorded in the Gulf of Anadyr. In Bristol Bay, storm surges have flooded the village of Togiak several times by raising sea level by six to nine feet (2-3 m). At the head of Togiak Bay a large cargo barge rests in the tundra more than a mile from the water's edge, where it was deposited by a fall storm surge during the early 1990s.

The U.S. Coast Guard cutter *Storis* slashes its way through some heavy weather on a Bering Sea patrol.

Climate and weather

The climate and weather of the Bering Sea result from large-scale atmospheric circulation patterns and from the tracks of pressure cells over both the sea itself and adjacent waters and lands. Much of the Bering Sea's weather originates over the North Pacific Ocean, and some over continental Russia. Locations of the Aleutian Low and the Siberian High "fix" the general weather pattern and account for much of the year-to-year variation in climate.

The Aleutian Low and Siberian High are not individual pressure cells, but rather are names given by meteorologists to the time-averaged locations of storms, or individual pressure cells. The Aleutian Low is the atmospheric pressure system that exerts the most influence on the northeast Pacific during the winter. The Aleutian Low Pressure Index (ALPI) is a measure of the geographical area of pressure (below 100.5 kPa) and is a good indicator of climate and ocean interactions in the Bering Sea.

Lows are associated with *cyclonic* winds (counter-clockwise in the Northern Hemisphere). For more intense lows, the spacing between the *isobars* is closer (isobars are lines connecting points of equal atmospheric pressure), and the wind is more intense. Lows tend to form south of Kamchatka and travel in a northeastward direction, either up the Aleutian chain and Alaska Peninsula, or up the center of the Bering Sea. About six to nine of these lows pass over the sea in a typical month, with the number

Ice from the Bering Sea.

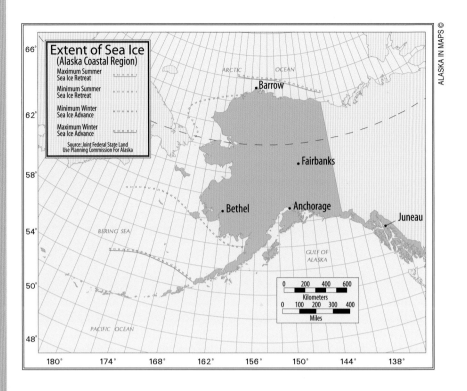

Extent of Sea Ice
(Alaska Coastal Region)

Maximum Summer
Sea Ice Retreat

Minimum Summer
Sea Ice Retreat

Minimum Winter
Sea Ice Advance

Maximum Winter
Sea Ice Advance

Source: Joint Federal State Land
Use Planning Commission For Alaska

ARCTIC   OCEAN

• Barrow

• Fairbanks

• Bethel   • Anchorage

Juneau

BERING SEA

GULF OF
ALASKA

0   200   400   600
Kilometers
0   100   200   300   400
Miles

PACIFIC OCEAN

The Bering Sea's seasonal ice advance typically covers the greatest area of any arctic or subarctic ice advance in the world.

increasing to 11 to 14 per month in spring and fall. The most intense lows are in the winter.

During the winter many of these systems track farther south and therefore they produce a combination of northwest, north, and northeast winds, with average wind speeds of 30 to 40 knots over open water and less in coastal areas.

When the Aleutian Low is located to the east, it brings warmer Pacific air into the Bering Sea region, resulting in a warmer winter. When the Aleutian Low is far to the west, the winter tends to be colder than normal. In the Bering Sea winter air temperatures range from above freezing to as low as –60°F (–51°C). Winter precipitation is only a couple of inches in the north, and as much as six to eight inches (15-20 cm) in the Aleutians.

During the summer some low-pressure systems develop over the Siberian mainland, and tend to track due east to the coast and Bering Strait. These systems produce west or northwest winds over the Bering Sea. They produce mainly south and southeast winds, averaging 10 to 15 knots. Air temperatures average 45-52°F (7-11°C) in the north and 51-54°F (11-12°C) in the south. Monthly precipitation averages one to three inches (2.5-7.5 cm).

Sea ice

Along with the broad continental shelf, the other defining characteristic of the Bering Sea is its seasonal ice covering. The two are tied together in that ice tends to form over the continental shelf and not form over the abyssal depths.

The Bering Sea's seasonal

This is an aerial view of sea ice on the Bering Sea. Although sea ice is made from salty seawater, the tight crystal structure of ice prevents salt molecules from staying in the ice. When the ice melts, it is freshwater, not salt water.

ice advance typically covers the greatest area of any arctic or subarctic ice advance in the world. This is due to the extreme cold air that sweeps in from the polar region and off continental Russia from Siberia. Driven by the Coriolis force (movement influenced by the rotation of the earth, to the right in the Northern Hemisphere), the air super-chills the sea's surface. Ice is less likely to form over the deep ocean basin because it serves as a heat sink (stores heat during the summer), and warmer water rises to the surface along the continental shelf or comes from the depths due to wind-caused upwelling.

Sea ice advance

Sea ice typically starts its advance in November in the Chukchi Sea and works its way through the Bering Strait and south in the Bering Sea. A small amount of sea ice on the Bering Sea comes from ice that is pushed south by north winds. But most of the sea ice *forms* in place, meaning that the sea surface cools to the point that pizza-size ice *pans* form to create a slushy covering, then the pans freeze together to form large plates or *floes*.

Cold air is *advected* (transported laterally) southward from the dense pool of polar air by the rising of slightly warmer air over the deep sea, causing strong, frigid north winds that push sea ice to the south. Ice also forms in place off the downwind side of islands, at the edges of *polynyas* (areas of ice-free water that occur on the lee sides of islands or other topographical features that break up the predominating north wind).

Cold air super-chills the surface of the sea and ice forms. But as it does so, winds blow it out of the polynyas and into the forming ice pack downwind. In fact, large polynyas off St. Lawrence, Nunivak, and St. Matthew islands and in areas of the Yukon Delta, Norton Sound, and Gulf of Anadyr, are major ice-making machines for the Bering Sea. While polynyas generate ice, the water in them remains open and provides habitat for air-breathing animals like marine mammals and seabirds.

The ice front advances to the south as the surface cools until eventually it meets warmer water, where the ice begins to melt. The meltwater cools the upper layer of the ocean, allowing more ice to form, and advancing the ice edge to the south.

The formation of ice breaks up wave action and stills the sea surface, and eventually the floes are welded together by the searing cold to yield an almost continuous surface of ice. From an airplane flying over the continental shelf in mid-winter, the sea ice can look almost like a cracked, slightly opaque pane of glass. This ice pack is relatively thin, most of it between four inches and four feet thick (10 cm-1.3 m).

Pan ice on the Bering Sea.

Declines in sea lions, seals, and numerous species of seabirds and forage fish all correlate with atmospheric pressure and temperature changes.

Year-to-year variation in ice coverage has always been the rule, with some winters exhibiting much more extensive ice coverage than others. The extent of sea ice covering is a function of the severity of the winter, and the location of major atmospheric low-pressure cells that generate storm winds and waves. When the Aleutian Low is farther west, atmospheric circulation brings cold air from the north, which promotes ice formation and increases the ice-making function in the polynyas.

In years when the Aleutian Low is strong, warm air is pushed northward and sea ice does not advance very far south. Also, during *El Niño* years the extent of winter ice coverage sometimes is dramatically less than "normal." El Niño is a periodic climate anomaly that starts in the tropical Pacific Ocean and can bring unusually warm weather to the North Pacific and even the Bering Sea.

A long-term reduction in sea ice coverage in the Bering Sea, starting in the early 1970s, coincides with big increases in the abundance of some species—like salmon and pollock—while other species began a long-term decline. Declines in sea lions, seals, and numerous species of seabirds and forage fish all correlate with atmospheric pressure and temperature changes. Air temperatures in Interior Alaska also have increased at the same time. Scientists have correlated this *regime shift* with changes in the atmospheric pressure index over the North Pacific. A regime shift is a change in the relative importance of species in an ecosystem. Scientists use the term *climate forcing* for the effects of broad-scale changes in weather patterns, such as big changes in sea life populations.

In mild winters the Bering Sea ice edge meets the Alaska coast near Kuskokwim Bay. During severe winters the ice edge reaches the coast near the western end of the Alaska Peninsula. On average the ice edge reaches to Ugashik in Bristol Bay. The edge tends to angle to the northwest, approximately along the same line as the continental shelf. On the Russian side, the ice forms from the coastline to the outer edge of the narrow continental shelf, and in some years it forms almost to the southern end of the Kamchatka coast. The thickest sea ice forms on the Bering Sea's western side.

Sea ice retreat

By early April each year the sea ice has begun to retreat. At this point, three and a half months after the time of minimum *insolation* (heat input from the sun), ice covers one-third to one-half of the Bering Sea, including three-fourths or more of the continental shelf. The nearly continuous covering breaks up into smaller floes, and the floes begin to melt and to dissolve in the wind through *sublimation*, which means to evaporate from the solid to gaseous state without becoming liquid.

At this time the ice looks "punky" or "rotten" and the flat floes become destabilized and tip or lie lopsided in the water. As spring advances the winds shift to the south and east and waves build up, further breaking up the ice. Wind and currents push the broken floes into *windrows* across the surface of the sea. While in the process of melting, much of the ice along the Alaska coast is swept northward by the Alaska Coastal Current and some eventually is flushed out through the Bering Strait.

The ice usually is gone from Bristol Bay by late April, although river ice may appear in bays until the rivers have "gone out" in late May, and some years ice remains in Norton Sound into June. The time of maximum ice retreat is September, three months after the time of maximum insolation, summer solstice. By September the ice edge normally has retreated well into the Chukchi and Beaufort seas.

River ice, which forms in the rivers and on the freshwater lens lying over saltwater in bays and near river mouths, is different from sea ice. Ice forms in the bays and at river mouths because freshwater has a higher freezing point, and because of cold winds that come down the valleys from the interior. When river ice begins to "break up," current moves it downstream. The ice frequently forms blockages or "dams" and when those let go huge volumes of river ice may be flushed into the sea within a short time. It can be a dramatic sight, but is not directly related to the advance and retreat of sea ice.

Salt lowers the freezing

April 22, 2002 — June 3, 2002

Bering Strait

Russia — Alaska

Top—These satellite images show the ice retreat in the Bering Strait as summer approaches. Bottom—This image shows pan ice as the ocean current flushes it southward from the Bering Sea through the Bering Strait into the Chukchi Sea.

point of water. This means that seawater freezes at a lower temperature than freshwater. When seawater freezes, the brine is extruded from it, so the ice itself becomes fresher while the sea around and below the ice becomes saltier. This seasonal creation of concentrated brine influences seawater

temperature stratification, nutrient mixing, and biological production. As discussed in Chapter 3, certain types of single-celled algae thrive on the underside of sea ice, and their spring blooms boost the explosion of life that contributes to the Bering Sea's remarkable biological productivity.

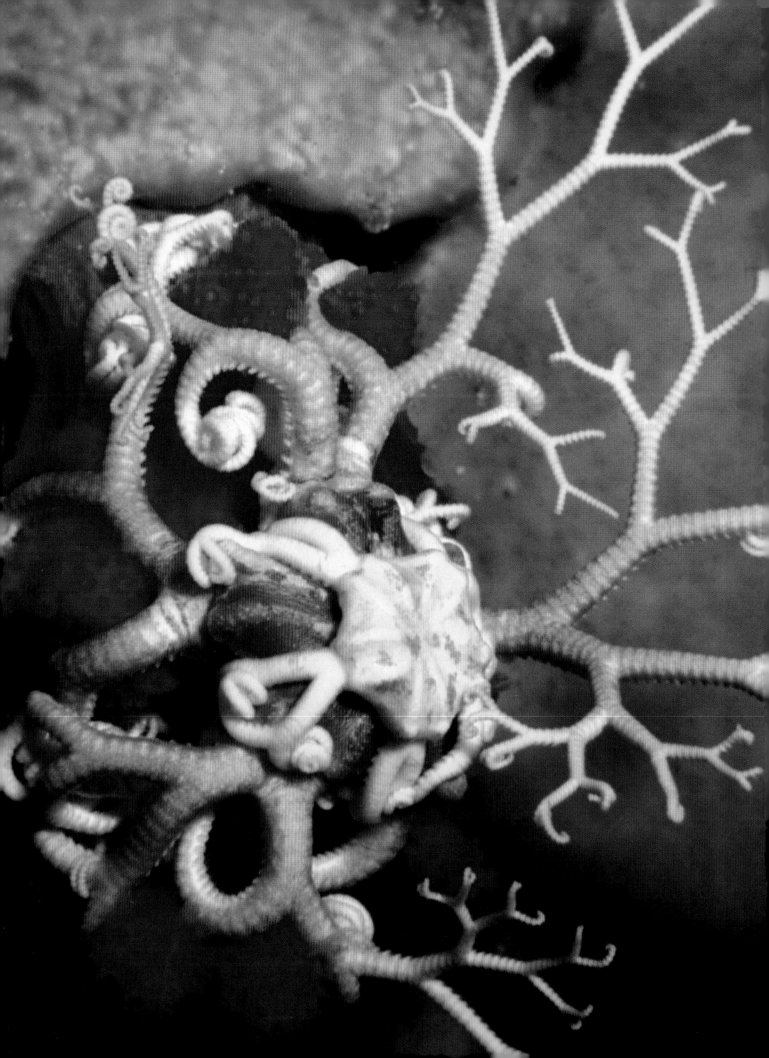

Life in the Sea
CHAPTER THREE

The foundation of the Bering Sea's food web, which supports all fish, birds, and mammals in the sea, is a large group of very small *microalgae*, microscopic organisms called *phytoplankton* (Greek for "wandering plant"). At key times and in particular places they are remarkably prolific. Scientists have identified 266 species of phytoplankton in the Bering Sea. Like plants, most phytoplankton employ the process of *photosynthesis,* the first step in using the sun's energy to convert nutrients into living plant material. They absorb carbon dioxide and give off oxygen—in fact oceanic photosynthesis is one of the most important sources of atmospheric oxygen. Photosynthesis and other life processes in the Bering Sea are limited by the availability of sunlight and nutrients.

Algae, including phytoplankton, were at one time classified as plants because they conduct photosynthesis. But they differ from terrestrial plants and biologists now classify them as *protists*. Protists comprise one of the five biological kingdoms, along with procaryotes, plants, fungi, and animals. There are about 30,000 species of protists, most of them single cells only hundredths of an inch across. The smallest, called *picoplankton*, are about one-thousandth of an inch in diameter. In some species each individual grows a hard shell made of calcium carbonate or silica. Some species of larger plankton (still less than 1

STEPHEN JEWETT/UAF ©

Sponges, sea stars, soft corals, algae, and other organisms populate the rocky seafloor at Amchitka Island.

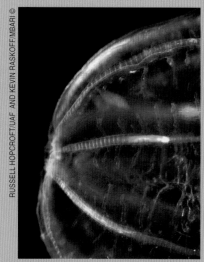

Closeup view of a microscopic comb jellyfish.

mm or a 25th of an inch in diameter), called *dinoflagellates*, have tiny whip-like tails or paddles and actually propel themselves through the water. Other protists include protozoans, amoebas, slime molds, and the multicellular brown algae such as most "kelps" or "seaweeds."

Most organisms in most ocean systems inhabit the upper 300 feet (100 m) of the water column, because this is where sufficient sunlight is available to activate photosynthesis, which drives the entire food web. Because of the broad, shallow continental shelf, much of the Bering Sea is within this productive zone.

The great profusion of plant and animal life begins on the cold underside of the ice pack in the northern Bering Sea. Phytoplankton, specifically *diatoms,* live there and grow slowly until the ice melts in the spring. When the ice melts the diatoms capture the abundant springtime sunlight to conduct photosynthesis and use nutrients (nitrates, phosphates, and silicates) brought up from the bottom and from the ocean basin by tide, currents, and wave action. In the shallower waters nutrients in the water column become depleted, unless more are transported into the area.

The meltwater from the ice pack establishes a surface layer of cold, less salty water floating on top of the denser seawater, and this is where the plankton prosper.

The aqua area in this satellite remote sensing image represents a plankton bloom in the Bering Sea.

Plankton blooms

The warmth of the sunlight causes a temperature *stratification* (layering) that creates ideal bloom conditions when nutrients are present. When environmental conditions are just right, the tiny plants rapidly reproduce, triggering a *plankton bloom* that turns the seawater brown. Later in the spring, summer, and fall, photosynthesis continues but the species of phytoplankton may change several times, in a process known as *succession*. For instance, the initial bloom of large diatoms may disappear to be replaced by dinoflagellates followed by small diatoms.

The way the water column is stratified, in temperature and salinity, both enhances and limits phytoplankton productivity. The meltwater from the ice pack establishes a surface layer of cold, less salty water floating on top of the denser seawater, and this is where the plankton prosper. The water is about 30°F, and at this temperature a massive bloom can occur in about one week. But if the layer is too shallow or if wind mixes the ice melt with water from lower in the water column, the bloom may be delayed and may develop slowly. Strong stratification can produce intense blooms of short duration that contribute little to the total production of the sea for that year. The ice edge bloom that advances north behind the retreating ice is followed by a water column bloom as the water warms.

The blooms of *pagophylic* (ice loving) phytoplankton give

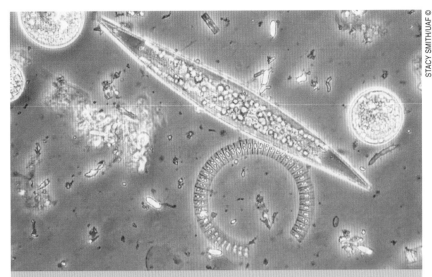

Diatoms, like these from the Bering Sea, sustain the base of the food web.

the seasonal *primary productivity* a head start of two to three weeks over non-ice-covered waters. However, because relatively few *zooplankton* live in these cold waters early in the spring, a lot of the phytoplankton material sinks to the bottom. It supports communities of *benthic* or bottom-dwelling plants and animals. The young of commercially valuable fish feed on it, as do larval crabs on the bottom. In cold years when the ice has advanced farther than normal, the spring bloom makes more food available in the system, and crabs in particular do well. On the other hand, the advanced ice with additional food is less of an advantage to pollock, since they spawn on the continental shelf and are less successful when the water there is colder.

Vertical mixing

Strong tidal currents meeting the steep shelf break bring nutrient-rich waters up from the abyssal depths via *upwelling* to the *euphotic* zone, where sunlight is plentiful. Photosynthesis occurs in profusion there during the summer. Currents along the shelf and across the northern shelf distribute nutrients across much of the northwestern part of the sea, allowing for a growing season that extends well beyond the spring bloom. The bloom quickly depletes nutrients in the upper water column over the continental shelf. The nutrients are replenished through upwelling at the shelf edge along with vertical wind mixing of the surface water by summer storms.

Ecological zones

The Bering Sea is composed of distinct ecological zones or *domains*, each of which supports key components of the complex food web. The *coastal domain*, which covers much of the shallow continental shelf adjacent to the Alaskan coast, is moderately productive.

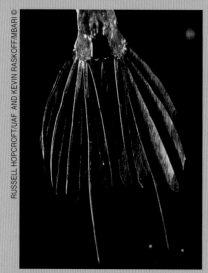

Tail of a copepod.

A single teaspoon of seawater is said to contain up to a million bacteria and ten million viruses.

The *middle* and *outer domains*, where the shelf starts to slope off to nutrient-rich deep water, is where plankton activity really revs up. The current flowing to the northwest is loaded with nutrients (nitrogen and phosphorus) that maintain a high level of plankton production. So much nutrient is available that it isn't all used as it passes over the shelf; therefore it contributes nutrients all the way up into the Chukchi Sea.

The Green Belt

The most productive zone—the shelf edge domain or *Green Belt*—forms a sweeping arc, from just north of Unalaska, following the shelf break northwest almost to Cape Navarin in Russia, and then down the rim of Karaginsky Bay and to the east coast of Kamchatka. At the apex of the arc, off the Gulf of Anadyr, a spur of the Green Belt extends north, loops in between St. Lawrence Island and the Chukotka Peninsula, and extends north again through the Bering Strait and into the Chukchi Sea. The area around the Pribilofs also is very rich, due to the influence of a large undersea canyon and tidal retention of rich waters and plankton.

Eddies are important in moving nutrient-rich water onto the shelf. The Green Belt includes numerous isolated productive patches where upwelling brings nutrients to the upper layer into sunlight. The water column in these areas is stabilized by coastal waters, which keeps phytoplank-ton high in the *euphotic zone* where blooms are produced. Strong primary productivity can extend down 60 to 100 feet (20-30 m) from the surface.

Phytoplankton blooms constitute *primary production*, and provide the food required by microscopic animals called *zooplankton*. The proliferation of zooplankton, of which there are 300 known species in the Bering Sea, is known as *secondary production*.

The microbial loop

It was long assumed that the flow of energy from sunlight through phytoplankton to zooplankton to carnivores was a direct line, a "food chain." Then in the 1980s scientists discovered that the amount of food reaching zooplankton was actually greater than phytoplankton production, taking into account losses from excretion and discharges. They developed a "food web" theory based on the concept that food was being recaptured, and even produced, by microbes. Bacteria and viruses, along with protozoans and small fungi, are the key players in this system, known as the microbial loop.

Bacteria and viruses, some of which cause disease, are extremely numerous in the sea. A single teaspoon of seawater is said to contain up to a million bacteria and ten million viruses. Bacteria perform several important functions in the marine environment—one is breaking down dead plant and animal tissue to release dissolved organic matter.

Bacteria also consume dissolved organic matter that has been discharged from photosynthetic creatures in a form that can't be eaten by low level protists, such as non-photosynthesizing flagellates. Because microbes are so microscopically tiny, their surface area to weight ratio is very high and they easily absorb dissolved elements from the water. Bacteria also are fed upon by grazing protists. Zooplankton, including these protists, play a major role in decomposition of organic material by feeding on detritus. Viruses don't break down dead organic material, but they add dissolved organic matter to the water by destruction of their host cells.

Whereas phytoplankton, such as diatoms, use solar energy to convert carbon into organic compounds, some kinds of microbes transform nitrogen, phosphorus, and sulfur into nutritionally useful compounds. Nitrogen is an important component of proteins and other biological materials, but much of the nitrogen in nature is unusable by most organisms. In a process called nitrification, bacteria manufacture nitrate and nitrite by breaking down ammonium and other nitrogen-based wastes. Cyanobacteria can convert unusable nitrogen into usable forms, and they are also photosynthetic.

It's now clear that between 30 and 50 percent of all biomass production at the lowest trophic levels in the sea is accomplished by bacteria, largely through recapture of dissolved organic matter that

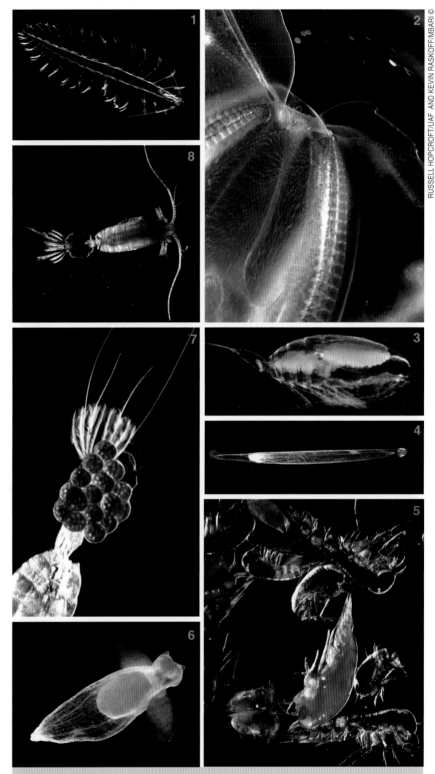

Bering Sea zooplankton. 1. Polychaete (pelagic worm). 2. Hydromedusae. 3. *Neocalanus* copepod with eggs developing inside. 4. Chaetognath (arrow worm). 5. Amphipods (sea fleas) and ostrapods (clan shrimps). 6. Pteropod (sea angel). 7. Large predatory copepod carrying eggs. 8. Copepod.

Medusae numbers gradually have increased in the Bering Sea, but in the 1990s their populations multiplied tenfold.

This commonly encountered jellyfish is called *Chrysaora melanaster*.

would otherwise be lost in the water. They are grazed by heterotrophic flagellates (phytoplankton-like organisms that eat organic compounds rather than photosynthesize their food), which in turn are fed upon by zooplankton.

Zooplankton

Principal among the zooplankton are copepods, tiny (a few millimeters) self-propelled creatures that are the key link between phytoplankton and the higher carnivores like fish.

They are important consumers of large phytoplankton and protists, making that energy and nutrient available to higher-trophic-level feeders.

Also feeding on phytoplankton are euphausids, commonly called krill, which are like tiny free-swimming shrimp (0.2-3 inches long, 0.6-8 cm) and are an important food for fish, birds, and some whales. Most species of euphausids are luminescent, or give off small amounts of light.

Cnidarians and amphipods also are zooplankton. Cnidarians are tiny soft sea animals like jellyfish. Amphipods are tiny crustaceans with legs and antennae.

Some kinds of zooplankton, especially protists and metazoans, are major decomposers of detritus in the sea. They regenerate dissolved inorganic nutrients through excretion of wastes from feeding on phytoplankton, bacteria, detritus, and each other.

Plankton concentrations can be astoundingly dense during blooms in the northern Bering Sea. Researchers have taken samples containing as much as 0.63 pound of living material per cubic foot of seawater (3 kg per cubic meter). Dense plankton blooms are visible from space.

The type of phytoplankton in the water can have a major impact on which zooplankton groups will find sufficient nutritious food. During spring, summer, and fall the varying food selections in the phytoplankton allow many zooplankton species to thrive. In turn they produce a variety of food items for the higher levels of the food web.

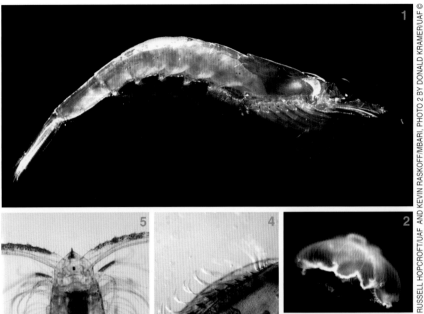

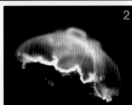
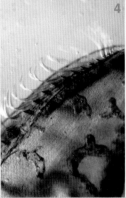

PHOTOS 1, 3, 4, AND 5 BY RUSSELL HOPCROFT/UAF AND KEVIN RASKOFF/MBARI. PHOTO 2 BY DONALD KRAMER/UAF ©

1. Krill. 2. Moon jellyfish, *Aurelia*. 3. Deep-sea comb jellyfish, *Beroë*. 4. Flagella of a plankter, used for locomotion. 5. *Neocalanus* copepod with mouth parts visible, used to eat other plankton. *Neocalanus* and other copepods are primary food for salmon smolt and other fish and invertebrates.

Jellyfish

The largest plankters are the *gelatinous zooplankton*, of which *medusae* or jellyfish are the best known. Some species are microscopic, others grow to nearly two feet (0.7 m) in diameter, weigh 25 pounds (11 kg), and have tentacles as long as ten feet (3.3 m). Medusae feed on copepods, other zooplankton, and fish eggs and larvae. In high abundance, they may have a limiting effect on fish populations.

Medusae numbers gradually have increased in the Bering Sea, but in the 1990s their populations multiplied tenfold.

The reason for this dramatic increase is not understood.

Although jellyfish and many other kinds of plankton have some ability to propel themselves short distances through the water, they have little control over their oceanic travels and are for the most part at the mercy of wave and current. The word "plankton" is from the Greek word for "wandering." Free-swimming crustaceans, some mollusks, plus fish and mammals, are called *nekton*, from the Greek for "swimming," because they can choose a direction and change their location.

Most pelagic fish migrate, in some cases over ranges of thousands of miles.

Rock and kelp greenlings are common in the Aleutians. This is a male rock greenling.

Fishes

Scientists have various ways of classifying fish; commercial fishermen, Native subsistence users, and other groups of people also have their own ways. In the simplest sense, there are finfish ("true" fish that swim with some variation on the familiar slithering motion), and shellfish. Shellfish are mollusks and crustaceans that lack an internal spine (*invertebrates*), and in most cases are covered by some kind of hard or spiny shell. Some are attached and sit nearly motionless on the bottom, some (like crabs) walk, and some (like squids) swim freely but with a different type of propulsive motion.

Among finfish, some are flatfish (halibut, flounder, and sole) and spend most of their time lying on their sides on the bottom. Although there are many dozens of species in Bering Sea waters, only a few, including halibut, some soles, flounders, and turbot, are familiar or of commercial value.

Most species are round fish and swim in an upright orientation, although some spend most of their lives on or in close proximity to the bottom. These latter are *groundfish* (commercial term), *demersals* (scientific term), or simply bottomfish.

Other groups of fish, known as *pelagic*, swim freely up in the water column or in close proximity to the surface. Most pelagic fish migrate, in some cases over ranges of thousands of miles. Within the broad category of pelagic fishes are groups that can be classified on the basis of how they fit into the food web.

Forage fishes

The key link between the microscopic and near-microscopic world of plankton and the larger, commercially valuable species, is a group of small fishes known as *forage fishes*. They are especially important because they are the dominant means of transferring energy from primary and secondary producers to the higher *trophic* level fishes, as well as to birds and mammals. Dozens of species of forage fishes and at least 16 species of squids have been identified in the Bering Sea. Most of them don't have names in English, but are known by Latin names only.

Most forage fishes are *pelagic schooling* species that aggregate in huge numbers and migrate around the ocean. They are small enough, average five inches long (13 cm), to be preyed upon by other fish and seabirds, yet all occur in densities great enough to make hunting them worthwhile for large mammals including sea lions and whales. Forage fishes include juveniles of several larger fish, such as pollock, herring, Atka mackerel, and even salmon. The number-one consumer of juvenile pollock is not sea lions, birds, or trawlers, but adult pollock. In the strictest sense, forage fishes include any fishes that are preyed upon by something larger.

Some forage fishes are predators on the juvenile forms of other species, and then become prey to those species as the individuals grow to adult size. For example, the adults of some smelts consume large amounts of juvenile pink salmon that are migrating from the rivers, yet young salmon feed on the juveniles of those same smelts, and adult salmon eat adult smelts. At the same time, smelts compete with the young salmon for food.

Mesopelagics

Many forage species are *mesopelagics*, for example lanternfish and deepwater smelts. Mesopelagics live in deep ocean waters down to 700 to 3,000 feet (250-1,000 m), where no sunlight penetrates. Because many of them make nightly (*diurnal*) migrations to the *epipelagic* zone near the surface, they are agents for redistributing organic materials into the euphotic zone. Some forage fishes are *bathypelagic*, or live at depths of 3,000-14,000 feet (1,000-4,500 m).

Mesopelagic fishes feed on larval and juvenile fish and zooplankton, and in turn com

SEA SCIENCE

UNIVERSITY OF ALASKA FAIRBANKS ©

A salmon attacks a school of Pacific sand lance in Prince Willam Sound, Southcentral Alaska.

Laser fish

It might seem strange to use an airplane to count fish, but that's just what scientists did in Alaska's Prince William Sound. On board the plane was a new technology tested by NPMR researchers that used lasers to gather images of forage fish. Called LIDAR (Light Detection and Ranging), it has been used for several years to measure cloud formations, and now it's being tested as a tool to count fish. Researchers say the technology will make counting fish easier and cheaper compared to traditional methods that use ships.

One of the most important of the forage fishes, both to other sea creatures and to human economy, is the Pacific herring.

A school of Pacific herring catches sunlight near the Pacific Ocean surface.

prise most of the food for some species of marine mammals. The forage species that are most familiar, however, and most accessible to other mammals, birds, and commercially valuable fishes, are pelagic and live at or near the surface. They include smelt, capelin, eulachon (or "hooligan"), sand lance, Atka mackerel, and herring.

Squids are not fish (they are *cephalopods,* which are *mollusks* and more closely related to clams than to fish) but they also are important forage animals. Fishing fleets of some Asian countries harvest them in the Bering Sea as a food resource. But their importance is far greater as forage for fish, birds, and marine mammals. An estimated four million tons of squid live in the Bering Sea.

Smelts

Five species of smelt live in the Bering Sea and in freshwater and brackish water systems along the coasts, and provide high nutrient feed to other sea creatures and to the people who live there. Largest is the rainbow smelt, called Arctic smelt in Asia. Individuals grow to a foot long (0.3 m) and a half-pound (230 g). The rainbow is a circumpolar species and commercially important in other parts of the world, though not in Alaska. The eulachon occurs only on the Alaska side and runs dozens of miles up *natal* rivers to spawn. It is the target of both commercial and subsistence fisheries in Alaska and British Columbia. The silver smelt of Asia and the pond smelt of Alaska are smaller and spawn in freshwater. The larger surf smelt spawns on ocean beaches on the Alaska side of the Bering Sea.

Subsistence fishermen catch smelts by fishing through the ice during late winter spawning runs and in open water at and near the mouths of rivers. All smelts are migratory and have high oil content in their flesh. In some areas eulachons are called "candlefish" because when dried and with a wick inserted they will burn like a candle. In some areas they are boiled to render "grease" which is used as a food supplement like seal oil.

Capelin

Closely related to smelt is the capelin, a fish that feeds and matures in the open ocean over the continental shelf and spawns in nearshore and intertidal areas in early summer. They enter the coastal zone only during the spawning season. Average size of adults is about six inches (15 cm) but they can grow to nearly a foot (0.3 m). Russian scientists have determined that five discrete populations live in the Bering Sea. In the North Atlantic and eastern Russia capelin is a commercial species, though it's not used in Alaska. Capelin are noted for undergoing dramatic changes in abundance; biologists believe that stocks in the western Bering Sea fluctuate by a factor of nearly 100 in the course of little over a decade. The scant information available on capelin abundance indicates their numbers have been very low since the early 1980s, but have increased in the late1990s.

Sand lance

Pacific sand lance is a small (3-11 inch, 7.5-28 cm) forage fish that normally lives close to the bottom in shallow water less than 300 feet deep (100 m). Sand lance form huge schools. Their distinguishing characteristic is that at night and during much of the winter they bury themselves, nose up, in sand to avoid predators and conserve energy. They constitute a major part of the trophic link between plankton and the larger fish and birds. Photos of puffins, kittiwakes, murres, and other diving birds often show the slim, silvery sand lance in their beaks. Sand lance also are food for salmon, cod, herring, and seals.

Pacific herring

One of the most important of the forage fishes, both to other sea creatures and to human economy, is the Pacific herring. Bering Sea herring grow big; older adult spawners average nearly a foot long (0.3 m) and nearly a pound in weight (454 g). The largest of many spawning

Top—Pacific sand lance wriggle out of the sandy Bering Sea seafloor where they embed themselves when not swimming in huge, dense schools. Like herring, sand lance in the Bering Sea are larger than in other regions, reaching lengths of 11 inches.

populations on the Alaska side of the Bering Sea returns each spring to Togiak in Bristol Bay. More than 100,000 tons, or between 200 and 300 million fish, arrive to spawn along the popweed-covered rocky shores each April and May. Other stocks spawn off the Yukon-Kuskokwim Delta and in Norton Sound. They reach the spawning areas just about the time the ice departs, and leave the nearshore areas in late summer.

Herring range over large areas of the Bering Sea and the adjacent Gulf of Alaska, and the American stocks mainly winter over the shelf in the Bering Sea just south

Pacific herring roe.

Individual halibut in the Aleutians have topped 400 pounds (182 kg), measuring more than seven feet long and five feet wide (2.3 x 1.5 m).

of St. Matthew Island. They feed on plankton and small fish, including juvenile salmon and, in turn, are preyed upon by adult fish, seabirds, seals, and other mammals. They are an important subsistence resource for coastal Native people, and are the target of a major commercial fishery. Their numbers fluctuate by as much as eightfold in decade-long cycles which appear to be associated with environmental conditions such as water temperatures.

Distribution and abundance of most forage species are not well known, but appear to be changing in response to environmental conditions, and in some cases to the effects of harvesting. Forage fish abundance may also reflect changes in abundance of those animals that feed on them, such as whales.

Bottomfish

Many fish species serve both as forage and as commercially important resources. The fish described here are most notable not for their role in transferring energy to higher trophic levels within the Bering Sea, but rather for their value as commercial resources and sources of food for a world of hungry humans.

Bottomfish include dozens of species that spend most or all of their time in close proximity to the sea bottom, almost all of it on the relatively shallow continental shelf. Some of these species, like pollock, cods, and some rockfishes, aggregate in huge schools and cruise up in the water column at least part of the time. Others, especially flatfishes, rarely relinquish contact with the seafloor except for short lunges to capture prey.

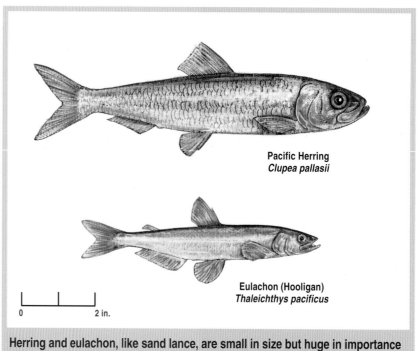

Pacific Herring
Clupea pallasii

Eulachon (Hooligan)
Thaleichthys pacificus

0   2 in.

Herring and eulachon, like sand lance, are small in size but huge in importance in the Bering Sea food web.

Pacific halibut

King of the bottomfishes is the mighty Pacific halibut, the largest fish in the Bering Sea (with the possible exception of some normally scarce and seasonally resident sharks). Individual halibut in the Aleutians have topped 400 pounds (182 kg), measuring more than seven feet long and five feet wide (2.3 × 1.5 m). Most landed commercially are less than 60 pounds (27 kg), which still makes them bigger than any other *teleost* fishes in the region. (Teleost fishes are bony, or "true" fishes, as opposed to *cartilaginous* fishes like sharks and rays.) The southeastern Bering Sea shelf is a major halibut nursery area for the North Pacific, and the average size there is smaller than in the Gulf of Alaska.

Halibut typically swim to shallower coastal waters to feed in the summer and return to depths of 1,000 to 1,500 feet in the winter (350-500 m). During the winter spawn each female releases up to two million eggs that drift with the current. A few months after the eggs hatch the larvae settle to the bottom and begin developing into small fish. Over a period of months the left eye "migrates" across the top of the head and settles next to the right eye. The fish turns over so its left side is down, and it turns white while the right (upper) side develops a mottled pattern that provides effective camouflage on sand or gravel bottom.

The halibut spends the rest of its life lying on its side or cruising slowly over the bottom snatching other demersal fishes,

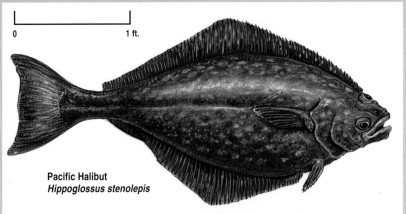

Pacific Halibut
Hippoglossus stenolepis

Top—A well-camouflaged Pacific halibut lies in wait for its passing prey. Halibut are voracious predators that seldom venture far from the seafloor.

crabs, octopus, or anything else it can get its jaws around. Halibut can live 40 years or more. The females get much larger than the males, exhibiting *sexual dimorphism* (males and females have different appearance). The populations of Pacific halibut, including those in the Bering Sea, increased substantially starting in the 1980s. Currently halibut catch levels on the American side of the Bering Sea and Aleutian Islands run about 13 million pounds annually (6 million kg) but are

expected to decrease over time as smaller year classes recruit into the fishery.

Flatfish similar to but smaller than halibut include Greenland turbot and arrowtooth flounder. Turbot and arrowtooth also inhabit shallower waters in the summer and return to the depths in the winter, when spawning occurs. Unlike halibut, they are considered low-value food fishes but are taken both in targeted fisheries and incidentally in nets set for other species.

Several commercial species, including arrowtooth flounder, rock sole, Greenland turbot, and yellowfin sole have been in decline for a decade or more.

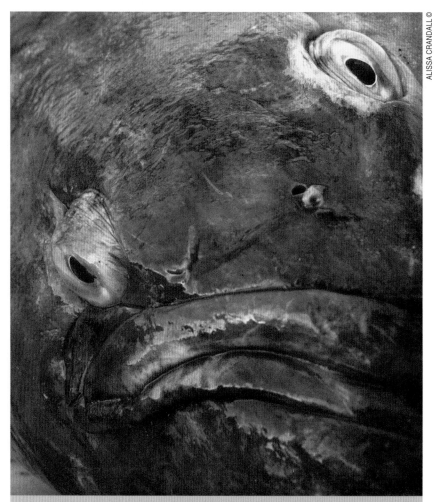

The world record sport-caught halibut, taken from the Bering Sea in 1996 near Dutch Harbor, weighed 459 lbs. Commercial fishermen have caught larger ones.

A number of other flatfishes occur and some are exploited commercially in the Bering Sea. Included are rock, yellowfin, flathead, rex, butter, and Dover soles, plus starry flounder, longhead dab and Alaska plaice. Probably most valuable is the rock sole, which is fished primarily for its valuable roe. It is most abundant on the shelf of the southeastern part of the sea where trawlers can catch them. Also heavily fished are the yellowfin sole, although access to some of the most productive grounds in Bristol Bay has been prohibited primarily to protect walrus habitat.

Both biomass and landings of flatfishes have fluctuated widely over recent decades. Catches have not necessarily reflected abundance trends, but instead have been influenced by regulatory and market considerations. Several commercially important species, including arrowtooth flounder, rock sole, Greenland turbot, and yellowfin sole have been in decline for a decade or more.

Sablefish

Most valuable of the round fish, on a per-pound basis, is the sablefish or blackcod. Not a cod at all, the sablefish has no close relatives in the North Pacific, but its succulent white meat is likened to butterfish and other tasty species of the tropics. It lives along the shelf edge in waters down to nearly 4,000 feet (1,300 m) but most are caught at depths of 300 to 3,000 feet (100-1,000 m). Average size is less than ten pounds (4.5 kg). They are called "silver cod" in Japanese and "coal fish" in Russian because the skin is a dark gray.

Cod

Several species of the cod family live in the Bering Sea. The tiny saffron cod is taken for subsistence only. Russian and Asian fleets harvest modest quantities of Arctic cod. The real prize of the family is the Pacific cod, a close relative of the Atlantic cod, and otherwise known to fishermen as P-cod, gray cod, or true cod. Some individuals grow to nearly 100 pounds (45.4 kg), and archeologists working in the Aleutians have found bones from cod that reached nearly 200 pounds. Cod live on the shelf in waters to a depth of 800 feet (270 m) and migrate between the shelf and the slope. They have excellent eating qualities and were the target of Alaska's first true commercial fisheries in the mid–nineteenth century. Trawlers, longliners, and pot-fishing boats continue to target cod for sale into Asian, American, and sometimes European markets.

Top—A technician displays a sablefish (blackcod). Middle—A Pacific cod hugs the seafloor near Adak in the Aleutian Islands. Bottom—A technician displays an Atka mackerel after tagging it and before releasing it back to the sea near Adak.

Adult pollock form dense schools, some of which may be hundreds of yards wide and deep, and miles long.

A male Atka mackerel guards a nest of eggs in about 75 feet of water near Seguam Island in the Aleutians.

Atka mackerel

Atka mackerel is a schooling *pelagic* fish (that is, it spends most of its time up in the water column rather than on the bottom) that is commonly lumped in with bottomfish. It is in the greenling family and not related to any mackerel. A small fish, averaging less than five pounds (2.3 kg), it is both a forage fish and a commercially targeted species. Atka mackerel live on the narrow shelf along the Aleutian arc from Kamchatka to the Alaska Peninsula and beyond, and they are taken by trawlers in waters of less than 250 feet (85 m).

Pollock

The walleye pollock is also in the cod family. It is far and away the most important of the Bering Sea's groundfish species, in terms of both commercial value and total contribution to the marine food web. Looking like a small, skinny cod, the pollock supports the single largest volume fishery in the United States and makes up about half of the bottomfish biomass of the Bering Sea. They inhabit the entire shelf and slope area out to depths of 1,500 feet (500 m) and may be found anywhere in the water column.

They spawn in shallower waters of 300-450 feet (100-150 m). Adult pollock form dense schools, some of which may be hundreds of yards wide and deep, and miles long. Larvae and juveniles constitute an important part of the forage fish biomass that feeds a whole range of larger fishes, birds, and marine mammals.

There are likely four separate pollock stocks in the Bering Sea, including one or more that spawn, rear, and mature on the narrow shelf of the Russian coast. Others are thought to spawn off the western Aleutians, off Bogoslof Island in the eastern Aleutians, and on the U.S. continental shelf.

Pollock appear to migrate over large expanses of the sea and evidence suggests that fish hatched and reared in the U.S. zone are taken by trawlers in the central Bering Sea (the "Donut Hole") as well as within the Russian economic zone and even its territorial waters.

Although classified as bottomfish or groundfish, adult pollock spend much of their lives up in the water column and can easily migrate across the abyssal depths of the Aleutian Basin.

Despite U.S. and Russian commercial fisheries of something like two million metric tons a year, pollock stocks are strong and appear still to be increasing in U.S. waters. However, Russian fishery biologists are concerned that their stocks are seriously depleted and in need of protection in the form of severe restrictions on fishing.

ART SUTCH ©

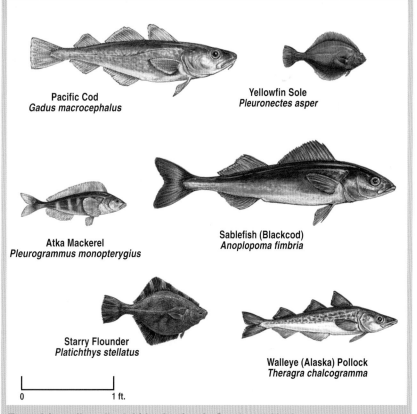

Pacific Cod
Gadus macrocephalus

Yellowfin Sole
Pleuronectes asper

Atka Mackerel
Pleurogrammus monopterygius

Sablefish (Blackcod)
Anoplopoma fimbria

Starry Flounder
Platichthys stellatus

Walleye (Alaska) Pollock
Theragra chalcogramma

0   1 ft.

**Top—A juvenile pollock bides its time in Southeast Alaska waters.
Bottom—Common commercially important groundfishes of the Bering Sea.**

Most rockfishes are found on or close to a rocky bottom, and many species do not form dense aggregations that would support commercial fisheries.

A sharpchin rockfish takes cover in red tree coral in the Aleutians.

Rockfishes

Several species of rockfishes inhabit the Bering Sea, the most abundant of which is the Pacific ocean perch (POP). Stocks are more abundant around the Aleutians, at depths of more than 1,000 feet (300 m), than on the shallow continental shelf. They are a schooling rockfish, susceptible to intensive harvesting by trawl gear, and like yellowfin sole their stocks were decimated by foreign fleets in the 1960s. Surveys indicate that the Aleutian Islands biomass of POP was depleted by more than two-thirds between 1960 and 1975 and has only partially recovered. Like most deep water rockfishes they are pale red in color, bear live young, and are extremely long-lived if not taken in the fisheries. Less is known about other rockfishes in the Bering Sea, including the yelloweye (although not a snapper, it is sometimes called a "red snapper"), rougheye, dusky, northern, shortraker, dark-blotched, and others. Most rockfishes are found on or close to a rocky bottom, and many species do not form dense aggregations that would support commercial fisheries.

1. Northern rockfish swims amid soft corals. 2. Red-banded rockfish. 3. Shortspine thornyhead rockfish near Adak. 4. Rougheye rockfish, and in the background a Pacific ocean perch near Adak. 5. Black rockfish.

King (chinook) salmon.

On the Alaska side of the Bering Sea all five species occur, although chums predominate north of Bristol Bay.

Salmon

The Bering Sea's second most valuable group of fishes (after pollock) is salmon. Five salmon species inhabit Bering Sea waters, at least part of the year. All salmon ascend rivers to spawn and the young of all species except pink and chum spend a year or more in freshwater to rear to *smolt* size, which is when they leave the stream and take to the sea. The presence of a species depends on the availability of freshwater spawning and rearing habitat. For example, most sockeye salmon need a lake system for rearing.

Most salmon stocks on the Russian side are pinks, with lesser amounts of chum and coho. Kings are scattered, and the only significant sockeye run is in the Kamchatka River. On the Alaska side of the Bering Sea all five species occur, although chums predominate north of Bristol Bay. A sizeable king run ascends the Yukon River—some of those fish swim upriver 1,200 miles (1,900 km) to spawn in Canada—and a lesser one in the Kuskokwim River. However, the Bristol Bay sockeye run dominates production on the Alaska side with tens of millions of fish returning to the six major river systems that ring the bay.

While young salmon enter the Bering Sea when they leave their natal streams, and mature adults emerge from the Bering Sea when they return to spawn, not much is known about where they live between those times. For the most part they leave the Bering Sea to feed in the rich waters of the North Pacific south of the Aleutians. How long the young take to find their way out through the Aleutians, and how long the adults may spend inside the Bering Sea on their return is unknown. Returning adult sockeyes have been traced as they run up the north side of the Alaska Peninsula, thanks

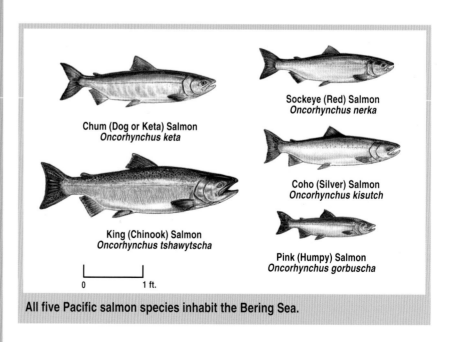

Chum (Dog or Keta) Salmon
Oncorhynchus keta

Sockeye (Red) Salmon
Oncorhynchus nerka

King (Chinook) Salmon
Oncorhynchus tshawytscha

Coho (Silver) Salmon
Oncorhynchus kisutch

Pink (Humpy) Salmon
Oncorhynchus gorbuscha

0   1 ft.

All five Pacific salmon species inhabit the Bering Sea.

to research by the University of Washington's Fisheries Research Institute. The institute does run timing and volume predictions, based on test fisheries off Port Moller. But for all other salmon stocks the migrations are at best only partially understood.

Alaska's Bering Sea sockeye runs hit their nadir in 1973 at about two million fish, subsequently rebounded to 40 million, and then settled back down to around 20 million. In most areas pink salmon, which have a two-year life cycle, experience a strong dominant

1. Completing their migration from the Bering Sea, these sockeye salmon are preparing to spawn in Iliamna Lake in Western Alaska. 2. King salmon (left) and two sockeyes head up the Karluk River on Kodiak Island to spawn. 3. Chum salmon return to a hatchery in Juneau. 4. Pink salmon in spawning phase on Kodiak Island. 5. Coho salmon near the end of their life cycle after which they will die and return nitrogen and other elements to the water to nourish future generations.

Golden king crab "face."

At least 150
species of clams,
crabs, shrimps,
anemones, sea
stars, sea urchins,
sea cucumbers,
sea onions, soft
corals, octopus,
and worms live on
the seafloor . . . or
burrowed into it.

year (either even numbered or odd numbered) depending on location.

Invertebrates

An astounding variety of invertebrates inhabit the Bering Sea. Some, such as crabs, attract the attention of human harvesters. But a great many more live their lives in quiet obscurity on the seafloor—that is, unless a 1.5 ton walrus or a 40-foot gray whale comes along, sucking up clams or dredging tons of bottom material to filter out the living contents of amphipods and crustaceans.

At least 150 species of clams, crabs, shrimps, anemones, sea stars, sea urchins, sea cucumbers, sea onions, soft corals, octopus, and worms live on the seafloor (called *epifauna*) or burrowed into it (*infauna*). Nearly all of them become the food of fishes, birds, and mammals.

King crabs

Three species of king crabs (red, blue, and golden), two species of Tanner or snow crabs, and hair crabs constitute the sea's most sought-after invertebrates. The red king or

Top—Rarely seen by humans, juvenile red king crabs mass into balls, called pods, during the day, probably as a "herding" behavior to protect themselves from predators. Bottom left—A king crab eats an urchin. Bottom right—King crabs engage in a mating grasp.

Life in the Sea

Kamchatka crab is the largest (individuals have a leg spread of as much as six feet [2 m]) and are the most widespread and abundant. During the 1970s they supported one of the most valuable commercial fisheries in the world, and remain a much-sought-after resource to fishing fleets on both sides of the Pacific. Red king crabs occur over the broad continental shelf in waters of less than 500 feet (170 m) although commercial concentrations are found mainly in waters less than 350 feet in depth (120 m). They are abundant on the narrower Russian shelf as well. Adult red king crabs feed offshore and return to coastal areas for spawning, and young remain in the shallower waters until they reach maturity. They eat mollusks, crustaceans, worms, and fish.

The smaller blue kings are abundant around some islands, including St. Matthew, St. Lawrence, and the Pribilofs. Golden kings, also known as brown king crab, are smaller still and prefer deeper waters, depths of more than 550 feet (180 m) along the continental slope and around the Aleutian Islands.

In the 1970s American fishermen developed the intense domestic king crab fishery (Russian and Japanese vessels had exploited the stocks for decades before) and after only a few years of intense exploitation the stocks crashed. Initially over-fishing was blamed, but subsequent research suggests a combination of factors including parasites, increase in the abundance of predators, and changes in water

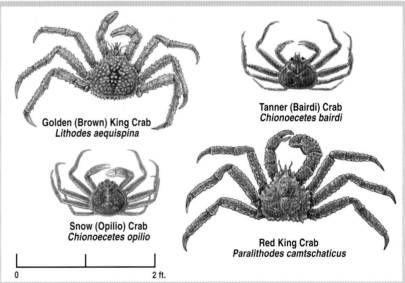

Top—A helmet crab, common in the Bering Sea, lurks in seagrass. Bottom—These four are the most sought crab species in the Bering Sea commercial fishery.

Golden (Brown) King Crab
Lithodes aequispina

Tanner (Bairdi) Crab
Chionoecetes bairdi

Snow (Opilio) Crab
Chionoecetes opilio

Red King Crab
Paralithodes camtschaticus

0   2 ft.

temperatures added to the effects of the fishery to cause the crash. Current landings are only a small percentage of the peak catches of 160 million pounds in 1980 (73 million kg).

Tanner, snow, and hair crabs

The Tanner (bairdi) crab and the smaller but more abundant snow (opilio) crab are smaller on average than king crabs but

big enough to attract commercial interest, and occur in much the same habitat as kings.

Tanner shell widths are six to eight inches (15-20 cm) and leg spread may be as much as four feet (1.3 m). Tanner and snow crabs, like all the species of king crabs, achieve maturity at about eight years of age. They are fished on the continental shelf and in the northern Bering Sea as ice permits. Like other crabs they exhibit large

Scientists estimate that there are more than 4 million tons of squid cruising the depths of the Bering Sea.

Juvenile Tanner crabs scuttle along the seafloor near Kodiak Island.

fluctuations in abundance—during the 1980s landings in excess of 300 million pounds (136 million kg) from American waters were recorded.

Korean hair crabs occur in a few locations and a small commercial fishery has operated out of the Pribilof Islands. The small crab has a horny, boxy shell and is covered with the bristles that suggest its name. During years of abundance they are caught and shipped live to markets in Japan. Catches peaked at about 2.5 million pounds in the early 1980s (1 million kg) but diminished thereafter, and some years the fishery doesn't even open.

Bivalve mollusks

Scallops are bivalve mollusks (similar to clams) that live on the sea bottom. Unlike other bivalves they can propel themselves through the water by ejecting a jet of water through their siphons. They are harvested for the succulent meat of the adductor muscle that draws the two halves of the shell together. They are filter feeders and live in beds containing large numbers of animals. Five species are in the region, with the weathervane the most important one. They occur from the intertidal zone down to about 1,000 feet (330 m) but are most abundant in 150-450 feet (50-150 m). The scallop fishery in the Bering Sea is small and intermittent, and depends on market conditions as much as resource availability.

A variety of clams live in intertidal and subtidal waters, including razor clams and several species of hard-shell clams. Large beds of surf clams occur on the continental shelf. Clams feed a huge biomass of walruses, but are unexploited by humans other than small numbers taken for subsistence. Paralytic shellfish poisoning (PSP), a nerve toxin

Life in the Sea

1. Small mussels cling to seagrass in Izembek Lagoon. Mussel densities get so concentrated on seagrass that their weight collapses the seagrass into mats on the lagoon bottom. The large concentrations of mussels also attract fish and crabs which voraciously feed on them. 2. Japanese abalone are found along the Russian Bering Sea coast, Japan, and Alaska south of the Aleutians. 3. Octopuses range throughout the Bering Sea and occupy a niche in the food web as both predator and prey. 4. The Bering Sea hosts 16 species of squid, important for forage. 5. One of several species of scallops that inhabit the Bering Sea.

produced naturally by marine bacteria and carried by a dinoflagellate, sometimes infects bivalves in the Pacific and renders them toxic to humans, but the scourge does not seem to occur in the Bering Sea. Nevertheless, clams and mussels go virtually unharvested, at least on the American side.

Squid

Sixteen species of squid play a key role in the Bering Sea food chain, in part because they are abundant and highly mobile. Scientists estimate that there are more than 4 million tons of squid cruising the depths of the Bering Sea.

Shrimps

Likewise, shrimps in the Bering Sea are little used by people. Several species have been identified, and the small pink shrimp is the most abundant. Few are taken commercially and not much is known about their biology in the Bering Sea.

In addition to the invertebrates that attract the attention of human harvesters, a great many more live their lives in quiet obscurity on the seafloor.

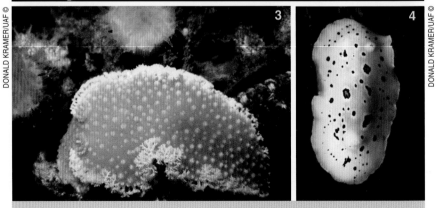

These are some of the colorful rock-dwelling animals that inhabit the Bering Sea–Aleutians seafloor. 1. A walking anemone near Shemya Island in the Aleutians. 2. Clown nudibranch, *Triopha catalinae*. 3. Orange peel nudibranch, *Tochuina tetraquetra*. 4. Spotted nudibranch, *Diaulula sandiegensis*.

1. *Pteraster* sea star near Shemya Island in the Aleutians. 2. Green sea urchins near Shemya. 3. Chiton, *Tonicella lineata*, near Shemya. 4. Sea star, *Henricia*, near Shemya. 5. Spawning sea stars, raised up to achieve maximum disseminaton of eggs and sperm. 6. *Pycnopodia*, a sea star common in the Bering Sea and throughout Alaska waters.

Tendrils of *Metridium*, a sea anemone.

Lush communities of invertebrates—including bryozoans, tunicates, sponges, hydroids, soft corals, urchins, anemones, sea stars, and more are characteristic of the rocky underwater habitat in the Aleutian Islands. These assemblages were recorded at Amchitka Island.

Life in the Sea

Left—Hydrocoral is surrounded by at least five species of sponges, near Adak Island in the Aleutians. Right—Bubble gum coral, *Paragorgia arborea*, amid hydrocorals, sponges, and hydroids near Adak. These photos were taken by a NOAA scientist aboard the submersible *Delta*.

Cold, old coral

Corals look like plants, but they are not. Corals in all their infinite variety are actually conglomerations of little animals that as a group take nutrition from the water around them and slowly grow as one.

Like trees on land, corals provide excellent habitat for many other animals. So when it comes to protecting underwater habitat, it's important to know how long corals live and how fast they grow.

Until recently no one knew how long corals in Alaska's deep, cold waters live. Using radio-chemistry, a scientific technique used to measure the rate of decay of naturally occuring radioactive elements within an organism, NPMR scientists calculated the age of red tree corals. Turns out, these far north corals grow very slowly, adding only about 2 cm of new growth each year. And the colonies live a long time, too. Scientists who measured one colony of red tree coral calculated their age to be more than 200 years.

Scientists gather information about the growth rate of corals that will help resource managers determine how to best protect underwater habitat.

Scientists display red tree coral from the Aleutians.

Humpback whale.

Marine mammals

The Bering Sea is unique in its profusion of marine mammals—at least 25 species. They are distributed very unevenly, with dense concentrations in some locations and entirely absent from broad expanses of sea. Some species of marine mammals currently are abundant, their numbers at or near historical highs. Others are on the endangered species list or are rarely sighted and little known to science. Some are abundant but are classified depleted or endangered because their numbers are lower than they once were. The Bering Sea's marine mammals continue to be important to the subsistence cultures of the region's Native peoples, and are significant attractions to both scientists and tourists.

Marine mammals are classified into three groups: (1) *cetaceans*, which include baleen whales, toothed whales, porpoises, and dolphins; (2) *pinnipeds*, which include earless seals (*phocids*), eared seals or *otarids* (sea lions and fur seals), and walruses; and (3) *marine fissipeds* (having separated toes). The only Bering Sea fissipeds are sea otters and polar bears.

Baleen whales

Most *mysticetes* or baleen whales are open-ocean travelers and feed on planktonic crustaceans and small fish, filtered out of big gulps of seawater that is expelled through plates of baleen in their mouths. Most baleen whales are seasonal visitors to the Bering Sea and depart into the Pacific as the ice begins to form. Some make long migrations to places like

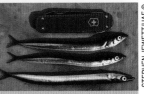

Baleen whales, like the humpbacks shown above "lunge feeding" in Southeast Alaska, are the world's largest animals. Massive as they are, they eat some of the ocean's most diminutive critters, especially krill (left), amphipods (middle), and small fishes including sand lance (right), herring, and eulachon. Bottom left and middle photos by Russell Hopcroft/UAF and Kevin Raskoff/MBARI©

Life in the Sea

Mexico and Hawaii each year for calving and return to the northern waters to feed. They include the biggest animals in the world—the blue whale grows to 90 feet (30 m) and 100 tons, and is spotted occasionally in offshore waters, as are the fin whale (70 feet, 23.3 m), the sei whale (46 feet, 15.3 m), the humpback whale (46 feet, 15.3 m), and the diminutive minke (26 feet, 8.7 m). All but the minke and the gray whale are on the endangered species list. Commercial whaling in the nineteenth and first three-quarters of the twentieth centuries diminished the stocks of most of the big mysticetes, and the total large whale population is now believed to be about fourteen percent of the pre-exploitation levels.

Bowhead whale

One baleen whale that does not migrate south from the Bering Sea is the bowhead. It migrates north, into the Chukchi and Beaufort seas as ice conditions allow during the summer. Although this 60-foot (20 m) mammal is endangered, traditional Eskimo hunting is permitted on a limited basis, mostly out of villages in the Arctic. About 7,500 range the Bering Sea part of the year. The long (6 foot, 2 m) feathery black strands of bowhead baleen are used in Native crafts and are frequently seen as decoration in homes and stores.

Right whale

An extremely rare baleen whale is the northern right whale, long believed to be absent from Bering Sea waters but now spotted

Top—A bowhead whale displays its distinctive white lower chin markings as it takes in air in the Bering Sea. Below the bowhead is a nice profile photo of a fin whale, clearly showing its dorsal fin, a distinguishing trait for whale identification. Bottom left—A blue whale, the world's largest animal, breaks the Pacific Ocean surface. Right—Whale tails, or flukes, are key for identifying cetaceans. Bottom right upper is a humpback fluke, bottom right lower is a fin whale fluke.

Once hunted nearly to extinction, the gray whale is a conservation success story, having rebounded to the pre-industrial hunting level of around 27,000 animals.

A gray whale evokes an ethereal presence in the Bering Sea.

there occasionally. It is not clear whether the right whale stock is recovering or has simply relocated. Similar in size and appearance to the bowhead, the northern right was hunted nearly to extinction. Whalers called it the "right" whale because it has desirable properties: it is slow and easy to approach, is high in oil content, and unlike some whales, it floats after being killed. Each year the National Marine Fisheries Service sends biologists out in airplanes to search for right whales, and some years they don't find any, so sightings by fishermen are the main source of information on their status.

Gray whale

One large baleen whale is not so rare—the gray whale. It migrates some 12,000 miles (19,000 km) round trip each year from the calving lagoons of Baja California to the rich feeding grounds in the Bering Sea and Arctic Ocean. Once hunted nearly to extinction, the gray whale is a conservation success story, having rebounded to the pre-industrial hunting level of around 27,000 animals. A mysterious die-off in the late 1990s reduced the stock by as much as a third, but the population appears to have stabilized. Cause of the die-off is uncertain but evidence points to insufficient

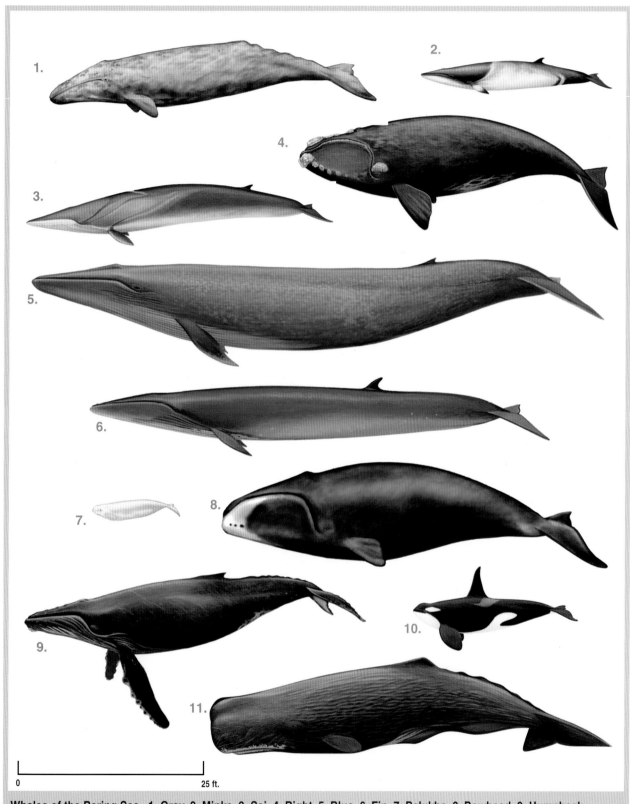

Whales of the Bering Sea. 1. Gray. 2. Minke. 3. Sei. 4. Right. 5. Blue. 6. Fin. 7. Belukha. 8. Bowhead. 9. Humpback. 10. Killer. 11. Sperm. Illustrations by Garth Mix.

MANDY MERKLEIN ©

A killer whale in the Bering Sea.

At 50 feet (17 m) and 40 tons the sperm whale is by far the largest toothed creature on the planet.

food possibly relating to the stock having reached and exceeded its carrying capacity.

The 30-plus ton gray whales are the only *benthic* (bottom) feeding whales, and meet their dietary needs by scooping up copious quantities of amphipod crustaceans and other invertebrates from the bottom by plowing it with their lower jaw and straining the food from the mud and sand. Like other whales, they pack on the pounds during a five-month feeding frenzy in northern waters, then go virtually without eating during the entire migration, mating, calving, and return trip. They favor shallow water and travel close to shore during the northward leg of their annual migrations. Sometimes they swim into tidal bays and lagoons and even a short way up shallow rivers. The much rarer Korean gray whale is occasionally spotted along the Kamchatka coast and probably enters the Bering Sea.

Aside from the gray whale, all the big whales are considered depleted, although little is known about either current or past populations. During the 1950s and 1960s thousands of large baleen whales were taken by commercial whalers in the Bering Sea, Aleutians, and Gulf of Alaska, including 15,000 fin whales, 5,000 sei, 1,500 blue, and 3,300 humpback whales. Current American estimates for the North Pacific, Bering Sea, and western Arctic Ocean put the grays at nearly 20,000 and fin whales well under 20,000. The combined total

Thar she blows!

In just one month-long cruise through the southeast Bering Sea in 1999, NPMR researchers counted 858 cetaceans, including one extremely rare and endangered northern right whale.

The scientists sailed from Bristol Bay to the Pribilof Islands. The most abundant species was the Dall's porpoise, 473 in 138 separate sightings. The next most-observed was the fin whale. Researchers counted 177 fin whales in 64 sightings. Also seen were humpback whales (11), minke whales (9), harbor porpoises (8) and killer whales (54). On one occasion, the observers spotted 125 Pacific white-sided dolphins traveling together.

The scientists conducted the research in conjunction with hydro-acoustical surveys of pollock stocks. During the survey, researchers scanned 198,000 square kilometers of ocean.

While whale numbers in the Bering Sea are still lower than during pre-commercial whaling days, the scientists think most whale populations are on the rebound.

of all other large mysticetes (blue, sei, humpback, right, and bowhead) is less than 20,000 animals. Russian estimates for these species are lower.

Toothed whales

The *odontocetes* or toothed whales are represented by two legendary ocean denizens, the sperm whale and the orca or killer whale. But there are a dozen other members of that family in the Bering Sea as well.

Sperm whale

At 50 feet (17 m) and 40 tons the sperm whale is by far the largest toothed creature on the planet. This behemoth of the seas developed something of a fierce reputation from the whaling days of old as a rammer of ships and sinker of small boats. Sperm whales travel in groups, roaming the oceans in search of squids and fishes. The blunt, squared head and row of conical white teeth in the lower jaw sets them apart from other large whales. At one time they were highly valued for the *spermaceti* (waxy oil) contained in their heads, and during the 1950s and 1960s commercial whalers took 26,000 sperm whales in the Bering Sea alone. They are primarily offshore whales but are seen occasionally inshore along the Alaska coast. Longline fishermen say that sperm whales sometimes lie alongside their boats when they are pulling gear, and some sperms have learned to strip

sablefish from the hooks as the fishermen retrieve their lines.

Killer whale

Even fiercer, at least by reputation, is the orca, or "killer whale." Though only 23-26 feet (8-9 m) and four to eight tons, they are known to rip apart much larger whales, sometimes apparently more for sport than food. They also kill and eat porpoises, sea lions, and seals. Scientists fairly recently have come to understand that there are two distinct genetically related groups of orcas. The *transients* travel long distances and prey mainly on other marine mammals, while the *residents* remain in smaller geographical areas, feeding almost exclusively on fish. The Bering Sea's orcas are predominantly the latter. Nevertheless, the eastern passes through the Aleutian Islands are known for a high frequency of orca attacks on large whales, and local people report seeing orcas kill

Top—Two killer whales cruise the Bering Sea. Bottom—Workers examine a juvenile killer whale washed up on a beach in Izembek Lagoon. Local people in villages on the Bering Sea coast have received training to help scientists study marine mammal strandings like this.

belukhas, walruses, and sea lions. Some scientists suspect that a drastic decrease in Aleutian Islands sea otter populations is due to predation by killer whales. The eastern Aleutians and southeast Bering Sea are favored orca hunting grounds and the overall population is several hundred.

Only 12-13 feet (4 m) and 1.5 tons, the belukha is the smallest animal commonly called "whale."

Belukha whale

Inhabiting bays and river mouths all the way around the Bering Sea coast are the little white toothed whales called belukha, often mistakenly called beluga. (Both names derive from the Russian word for "white" but belukha is the whale and beluga is the white sturgeon, a cartilaginous fish.) Only 12-13 feet (4 m) and 1.5 tons, the belukha is the smallest animal commonly called "whale." They hunt in the murky tidal waters with a type of sonar and catch fish in their small, sharp teeth. It is believed they can stun their prey with sharp blasts of sound. They travel and hunt in groups of dozens and even hundreds, and an estimated 25,000 live in the Bering Sea, adjacent bays, and the lower reaches of some tributary rivers.

Porpoises and dolphins

Three smaller relatives of the belukha also occur in the

Scientists estimate that the Bering Sea hosts more than one-third of the world's belukha population. Some of the whales are year-round residents, others are seasonal visitors. They tend to congregate near shore and in and around ice.

Bering Sea—Dall's and harbor porpoises, and the Pacific white-sided dolphin. The dolphin, at 7.5 feet (2.5 m), is the largest and the harbor porpoise is the smallest, at 5 feet (1.7 m). The dolphin is abundant in the Pacific but appears only rarely

Top—A pair of Dall's porpoises race in tight formation along the surface of the Bering Sea. Bottom—A Pacific white-sided dolphin exhibits typical "porpoising" behavior.

Beaked whales

Three species of rare beaked whales are occasionally found in the Bering Sea, including the Cuvier's, Baird's, and Stejneger's beaked whales. All three are believed to be denizens of the deep water at the shelf break and beyond, but otherwise little is known about their distribution and abundance.

Pinnipeds

In part because of their affinity to coastal areas, *pinnipeds* have been a bigger part of the subsistence economies of most Bering Sea Native peoples than have cetaceans.

All species of seals, sea lions, and walruses haul out on land or ice to rest and give birth to young, making them more accessible to hunters than most whales. Besides, a dead pinniped is a more manageable package than an expired whale, although a 1.5 ton walrus is also a pretty big chunk of meat to handle.

Most of the Bering Sea pinnipeds are ice-associated species, including spotted, ringed, ribbon, and bearded seals, and walrus, and some move in from the Chukchi Sea only with the fall ice advance.

They rest, mate, and bear young on shorefast or floe ice, in some cases traveling a thousand miles north and south as the ice advances and retreats. All but bearded seals and walruses are primarily fish eaters, and have evolved with special physiological adaptations for locating their prey in the

on the Bering side of the Aleutians, whereas the two porpoises are scarce north of the Aleutians but more widely distributed. All three eat small schooling fishes and squids. The harbor porpoise is slow swimming, shy, and usually appears alone or in small family groups. The other two are gregarious, fast swimmers, and often attracted to moving boats. Groups of dolphins sometimes include thousands of animals. Dall's porpoise is the most abundant with a population of perhaps 10,000 in the Bering Sea and Aleutians.

All phocids in the Bering Sea are ice seals except for the small harbor seal, which hauls out and pups on rocky outcrops or sandy beaches.

Harbor seals occur from Bristol Bay south on the American side of the Bering Sea.

cold, dark depths under the ice pack. Some, like the ringed seal, maintain holes in the ice that they use as access to the water below.

Seals

Phocids (seals) have no ear flaps. They lie prostrate on ice or land, and skootch along almost like a caterpillar when they need to move. But in the water they use a graceful fishtail motion of their hind flippers to propel themselves efficiently. All phocids in the Bering Sea are ice seals except for the small harbor seal, which hauls out and pups on rocky outcrops or sandy beaches. Harbor seals,

similar in appearance to the spotted seal, occur from Bristol Bay south on the American side. As many as 10,000 live in the southern Bering Sea.

Sea lions

Otariids (sea lions and fur seals) have external ears, and can rotate their hind flippers forward and prop themselves up on their fore flippers to shuffle over solid ground. Sea lions propel themselves through the water with a bird-like flapping motion of their oversized fore flippers. They can make great speed and even leap into the air if motivated.

Walruses

Walruses lack ear flaps and swim with a motion similar to the phocids, but have rotating hind flippers like the otariids. Walruses (weighing up to 1.5 tons) and the big bearded seals (500 pounds, 230 kg) are benthic feeders and eat clams, worms, snails, and other invertebrates on the seafloor. Walruses use their *vibrissae* (sensory organs on the snout which are evolved from whiskers) to locate clams buried just below the surface of the soft sand or mud. Then they grasp the bivalves in their lips and suck the contents out with a rapid motion of their piston-like tongues.

The huge ivory tusks, specially adapted upper canine teeth, are used primarily in mating displays and as ice picks to help them haul out on the floes.

Walruses were hunted commercially from the latter half of the eighteenth century until the 1990s. Since the 1960s stocks have rebounded and walruses are believed to be at or near the carrying capacity of their habitat, with about 200,000 animals.

Walruses were taken commercially, earlier by Yankee whalers who had depleted the Bering Sea's great whales, and more recently by crews from Soviet collective farms. The Soviet hunters took the ivory for crafts, the hides for industrial products like drive belts, the oil for industrial purposes, and the meat to use as feed in fox farms. Russian commercial walrus hunting ended in the early 1990s shortly after the demise of the Soviet Union.

ALISSA CRANDALL ©

FRED HIRSCHMANN ©

ALISSA CRANDALL ©

Top down—Harbor seals lie hauled out on the Katmai National Park coast. Walruses relax at Round Island near the Togiak National Wildlife Refuge.

Native people have unrestricted rights to hunt pinnipeds and belukha whales for subsistence purposes as long as the animals are taken in a non-wasteful manner.

A nothern fur seal pup rests on St. Paul Island in the Pribilofs.

The ongoing subsistence hunts, with an annual combined total of less than 10,000 animals on both sides of the ocean, are not considered to be a threat to the population.

Northern fur seal harvest

All kinds of pinnipeds are harvested for subsistence purposes, and some have been targeted in industrial fisheries in the past. Most notable was the huge northern fur seal hunt, on the Pribilof Islands and at sea, for much of the nineteenth and early twentieth centuries, which reduced the stock of three million animals by 90 percent. Tens of thousands of mostly young bachelor male fur seals were taken annually, initially by Japanese and Russians, and later by Canadian and American sealers. The Americans were mostly Aleuts, originally moved to the Pribilofs by Russian fur traders for the purpose of

[PUBLIC—No. 120.]

AN ACT to prevent the extermination of fur-bearing animals in Alaska.

Be it enacted by the Senate and House of Representatives of the United States of America in Congress assembled, That it shall be unlawful to kill any fur-seal upon the islands of Saint Paul and Saint George, or in the waters adjacent thereto, except during the months of June, July, September, and October in each year; and it shall be unlawful to kill such seals at any time by the use of fire-arms, or use other means tending to drive the seals away from said islands: Provided, That the natives of said islands shall have the privilege of killing such young seals as may be necessary for their own food and clothing during other months, and also such old seals as may be required for their own clothing and for the manufacture of boats for their own use, which killing shall be limited and controlled by such regulations as shall be prescribed by the Secretary of the Treasury.

SEC. 2. And be it further enacted, That it shall be unlawful to kill any female seal, or any seal less than one year old, at any season of the year, except as above provided; and it shall also be unlawful to kill any seal in the waters adjacent to said islands, or on the beaches, cliffs, or rocks where they haul up from the sea to remain; and any person who shall violate either of the provisions of this or the first section of this act shall be punished, on conviction thereof, for each offence by a fine of not less than two hundred dollars nor more than one thousand dollars, or by imprisonment not exceeding six months, or by such fine and imprisonment both, at the discretion of the court having jurisdiction and taking cognizance of the offence; and all vessels, their tackle, apparel, and furniture, whose crew shall be found engaged in the violation of any of the provisions of this act shall be forfeited to the United States.

SEC. 3. And be it further enacted, That for the period of twenty years from and after the passage of this act the number of fur-seals which may be killed for their skins upon the island of Saint Paul is hereby limited and restricted to seventy-five thousand per annum; and the number of fur-seals which may be killed for their skins upon the island of Saint George is hereby limited and restricted to twenty-five thousand per annum: Provided, That the Secretary of the Treasury may restrict and limit the right of killing if it shall become necessary for the preservation of such seals, with such ___ ___ reserved to the government as sha ___ ___ person shall knowingly violate eith ___ he shall, upon due conviction ther ___ provided herein for a violation of t ___ sections of this act.

Left—Within a decade after the United States bought Alaska from Russia and took over the Pribilof Islands and the fur seal harvest there, fur seal numbers dropped precipitously, threatening the lucrative industry. To restore the revenue stream, the U.S. Congress passed a law to restrict the annual commercial take to 75,000 seals on St. Paul, and 25,000 seals on St. George.

DIV. SPECIAL AGENTS,
FORM 17.

Island of St. Paul
BERING SEA, ALASKA.

August 18 , 1897

This is to certify that Eighteen thousand four hundred (18400) Fur-Seal Skins, have this day been shipped on board the Alaska Commercial North American Company's Steamer "Del Norte," Consigned to the North American Commercial Company San Francisco.

C E Allen
Master

Joseph Murray
Assistant Treasury Agent,
in Charge of the Seal Fisheries

Right—A receipt written in 1897 documents a delivery of seal hides to the Alaska Commercial Company, with whom the U.S. government contracted to transport the hides to San Francisco.

Bull and cow Steller sea lions.

Between 1959 and 1972, almost 46,000 Steller sea lion pups were legally harvested for their pelts.

This is an excerpt from a letter written in 1888 by William Gossitt, the U.S. Treasury agent in charge of the Pribilof Islands. Gossitt registers a plea with his superiors in Washington, D.C., to send him bombs or a Gatling gun to kill marauding orcas that were attacking and eating hundreds of fur seals as they approached the islands to breed. He also suggests that the meat and blubber from the "monsters" would be a welcome new source of food for the Natives. The weapons were not sent. This documentation of large-scale predation by killer whales on fur seals lends credence to current theories that suggest killer whales affect other marine mammal populations in the Aleutians and Bering Sea.

harvesting seals. Large-scale commercial sealing ended in the early part of the twentieth century after the stocks had become severely depleted, and a smaller government-sponsored hunt ended in the 1970s. Aleuts still take a few hundred fur seals a year in the Pribilofs for subsistence. Fur seal rookeries also are on the Kommandor Islands and on Bogoslof Island in the Aleutians.

Although numbers re-bounded after the hunt ended, the northern fur seal is classified as depleted under the Marine Mammal Protection Act. Numbers total over a million animals now, but counts have dropped in recent years.

Adult males weigh in at 300-600 pounds, while females are only one-fifth of that. Both genders spend most of their lives at sea, mainly in the northern Pacific and the southern edge of the Bering Sea.

THE SEA-LION HUNT ON PRIBYLOV ISLANDS.

Shooting the old males; spearing the surround; the drive.   (Sect. v, vol. ii, pp. 468, 469, 471.)

Drawing by H. W. Elliott.

Steller sea lions range throughout most of Alaska's marine waters, except the High Arctic. Top—Steller sea lions in the Bering Sea (left) and a bull and females in Southcentral Alaska (right.) Bottom—This is an artist's rendering from 1872 that depicts the process used in the Pribilofs to harvest Steller sea lions. Today Steller sea lions are protected by the Endangered Species Act.

They can dive to 180 meters (600 ft) to catch fish and squid.

Sea lion decline

The ubiquitous Steller (northern) sea lions range along both coasts of the northern Pacific and throughout most of the ice-free Bering Sea. But their numbers have decreased by more than 80 percent in a little over two decades.

Stellers are big animals, seven to nine feet (2.3-3 m) and 600 to 1,500 pounds (270-680 kg), and are opportunistic fish feeders. They haul out and pup on remote rocky islands and capes, and are not heavily hunted.

Commercial fisheries kill some either intentionally or incidentally. Between 1959 and 1972, almost 46,000 Steller sea lion pups were legally harvested for their pelts. Some 14,300 of those animals were taken from the Aleutian Islands and Bering Sea. That was the only commercial

All marine mammals are protected under provisions of the Marine Mammal Protection Act, and most under the Endangered Species Act.

A bull Steller sea lion surveys his territory on a beach at Amchitka Island in the Aleutians.

harvest of Steller sea lions.

Since 1972 they have been legally protected in American waters, yet their numbers have continued to decrease in the Bering Sea to only a few thousand. Some scientists believe that food stress, possibly related to patterns of commercial fishing or to climate change, is the cause. Others are looking at "top down" sources of mortality, such as orca predation, entanglement in fishing gear, and disease, perhaps in combination with dietary factors, as the cause.

Fissipeds

Two Bering Sea mammals are in the *fissiped* group—sea otter and polar bear. The sea otter is the largest (5 feet [1.7 m], 70 pounds [32 kg]) member of the weasel family. They rarely leave the sea, but eat, sleep, and nurse while floating on their backs in the ocean swell. They eat urchins, crabs, and clams. Since sea otters cannot survive where ice blocks access to food, in the Bering Sea they are found only at its southern margin, especially in the Aleutians. Having been nearly eradicated by Russian and Aleut hunters in the eighteenth and nineteenth centuries, they made a dramatic recovery. But in recent years their numbers in the Aleutians have again plunged. Predation by orcas, forced to change their diet due to the decline in sea lions, is a postulated but unproven cause.

Only a few polar bears enter the Bering Sea, while hunting seals on the ice floes in the Bering Strait area. Several thousand live in Alaska, and they appear frequently on St. Lawrence Island, but most of them are farther north in the Chukchi Sea and Beaufort Sea. The big white bears, up to 900 pounds (410 kg), spend their lives closely associated with shorefast and pack ice, and may range more than a hundred miles offshore.

STEPHEN TRUMBLE/UAF ©

STEPHEN JEWETT/UAF ©

BRENDA KONAR/UAF ©

Management

Sea otters, polar bears, and walruses are the three marine mammals in Alaska managed by the U.S. Fish and Wildlife Service. All others come under National Marine Fisheries Service authority. All marine mammals are protected under provisions of the Marine Mammal Protection Act, and most under the Endangered Species Act. Native people have unrestricted rights to hunt pinnipeds and belukha whales for subsistence purposes as long as the animals are taken in a non-wasteful manner. They also have limited quotas for hunting bowhead whales, and at Round Island in Bristol Bay they have a walrus quota. Other than bowheads and belukhas, Alaska Natives generally do not hunt whales. Chukchi Natives take gray whales along the Russian coast.

CARMEN FIELD ©

Top—Sea otters in the Bering Sea are most common in the Aleutian and Kommandor islands where kelp and sea urchins are plentiful.
Bottom—Polar bears occur in the northernmost part of the Bering Sea region.

While some kelps are *perennials*, meaning they live year after year, most are *annuals* and die after one season.

A rock greenling rests near the holdfast of a ribbon kelp alga.

Seaweeds and marine plants

The most conspicuous plant-like organisms in the sea are *macroalgae*, a large photosynthetic group known as seaweeds. They exhibit amazing variations on *morphology* (structure and form) and reproductive methods. Macroalgae belong to the kingdom *Protista*, and are more closely related to diatoms than to terrestrial plants and seagrasses. Macroalgae differ from "true" plants primarily by their (1) single-cell reproductive structures rather than multicellular structures such as stamens and pistils, and (2) lack of *vascular* tissue that transports nutrients around the plant (*phloem* and *xylem*). The entire macroalga is photosynthetic, not just the leaves.

While some kelps are *perennials*, meaning they live year after year, most are *annuals* and die after one season. A few, called *ephemerals*, live only a few months.

Names

Individual species of macroalgae have amazingly fanciful common names in the English language, including alternate skein, devil's apron, Bering membrane wing, bleached brunette, rock fuzz, red cellophane, bull whip, chocolate pencils, dead man's fingers, dragon kelp, feather boa, gooey golden seaweed, mermaid's glove, witch's hair, natasha's red blade, poor man's weather glass, rubber threads, splendid iridescent, and studded sea balloons.

Anchoring

All adult forms of macroalgae attach firmly to the sea bottom or to another surface such as a mollusk shell. This is in contrast to microalgae (phytoplankton) such as diatoms and dinoflagellates, which are mostly single-celled, microscopic, and drift free with the ocean currents. Free floating or beach-cast seaweeds don't live a transient lifestyle; either they were wrenched free of their grip on the bottom by wave and current action, or were cut through by grazing herbivores such as sea urchins. Much of the plant debris on beaches is dead kelp that broke loose after its structure was weakened by the start of decomposition.

Colorful sponges and ribbon kelp are some of the last holdouts against an onslaught of sea urchins that have eaten most of the organisms at this site near Shemya Island in the Aleutians.

Color

Most macroalgae, including the familiar, large seaweeds are in the phylum *Chrysophyta*, or brown algae, even though most appear more greenish than brown and some are red, black, yellow, or other colors. The color depends on the types of photosynthetic pigments. Macroalgae employ colored pigments in their cells to process and store nutrients. All algae employ the green chemical compound chlorophyll in photosynthesis, but they also have other pigments that alter their color. For example, red algae have *phycobilin*. This pigment absorbs light in deep water and allows red algae to grow much deeper than the greens and browns, sometimes to hundreds of feet. Some true green algae (phylum *Chlorophyta*) also are multicellular like the browns, but relatively few green algae live in the sea; most are freshwater or terrestrial species. All of the browns in the order *Laminariales* are commonly known as kelp.

Kelp structure

Kelps have three parts: a *holdfast* that grips a rock or some other bottom feature, a *stipe* that looks like a stem and connects the holdfast to the rest of the plant, and a *blade* which is where much of the sunlight collection and photosynthesis occurs. In most species the region of plant growth is located at the base of the stipe and base of the blade. Blades come in all sizes and shapes, many not resembling plant leaves at all but looking like twigs, flowers, hair, balls, or

Ribbon kelp at Shemya Island in the Aleutians.

Kelp communities are very diverse, containing hundreds of different species of invertebrates and fishes.

Sea urchins and ribbon kelp are common on rocky bottoms in the Aleutians.

sponges, in different species. In some the stipe is tiny or nonexistent and in others it is as long as 100 feet (33 m). Kelps do not have roots; they derive their nutrients from the surrounding seawater through the cell walls of the entire plant rather than from the soil or sea bottom.

Seaweeds in the food web

Macroalgae play an important role in the food web. They take dissolved nutrients from the seawater, capture solar energy, and through photosynthesis produce sugars that are made into plant tissue. When blade

Life in the Sea

tips slough off or when the plant dies and decomposes, that plant tissue is released into the water column or sinks to the bottom as *detritus* in forms that can be used by other sea creatures like filter feeders (such as clams and mussels) and invertebrates that live in, on, and near the bottom. Numerous invertebrates, including sea urchins, chitons, snails, and limpets specialize in feeding on kelps. The now-extinct Steller sea cow was a kelp eater, and a few terrestrial mammals like caribou and bears will feed on kelp under some conditions.

Besides providing food directly, some kelps provide a *canopy* or a thick mat or *turf* of plant material that shelters other plants and animals from predators and harbors their food. Kelp communities are very diverse, containing hundreds of different species of invertebrates and fishes. In fact, kelp holdfasts alone can be home to hundreds of brittle stars, worms, clams, and crustaceans. The kelp canopy is an important refuge for some commercial fish species for rearing habitat in their juvenile stages. In Bering Sea waters, the dominant canopy-forming kelps are *Nereocystis* (bull whip kelp) and *Alaria* (ribbon kelp).

Because kelps are attached to the bottom, and need sunlight to photosynthesize, most live in very shallow water. With few exceptions they are residents of the coastlines and shores of islands. In fact most are in or close to the intertidal zone, and for most species in northern waters the maximum depth at which they can live is 50-60

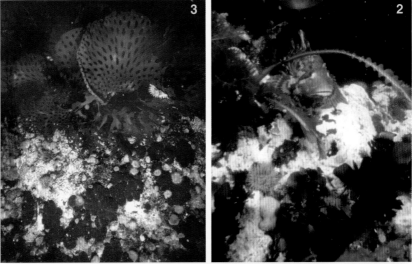

1. Sunlight filters through ribbon kelp in the Aleutians. 2. A greenling peers out from its ambush spot. 3. The alga *Thalassiophyllum clathrus*. 4. Ribbon kelp and sponges at Shemya Island.

Green sea urchins cover kelp stipes after eating the kelp at Amchitka Island.

In the Aleutians large kelps are part of an interesting dynamic that also involves sea urchins, sea otters and, it now appears, killer whales and sea lions.

feet (17-20 m). Below that depth too much of the sunlight spectrum is filtered out by water, sediments, and plankton blooms to allow growth. Besides, the hard substrate they need for attachment is lacking at these greater depths.

Most Bering Sea seaweeds are in the south

The Bering Sea is a fairly inhospitable environment for most kelps. Ice blocks sunlight and scours the intertidal zones. Silt deposits from rivers cover great expanses of shallow water, burying solid substrates like rocks that would serve as an anchoring point for holdfasts.

The southern rim of the Bering Sea, specifically the Aleutian and Kommandor islands, are rich in seaweeds, but the rest of the sea is much less so. At least 13 species of green algae, 29 species of brown algae, and 46 species of red algae live on the shores of those rocky islands. But only about four greens, eight browns, and 18 reds have been noted farther north in the Bering Sea. Not only is species diversity less, but plant density also is less.

In the Aleutians large kelps are part of an interesting dynamic that also involves sea urchins, sea otters and, it now appears, killer whales and sea lions. A major predator on kelps is the sea urchin, and the major predator on sea urchins is the sea otter. When otters were scarce, having not yet rebounded from the large-scale commercial harvests in the late nineteenth century, urchins

were abundant and kelp beds small and patchy. As otter populations grew they cropped the urchins and the kelp beds expanded.

For decades, extensive beds primarily of *Alaria* (ribbon kelp) and other species surrounded much of the shoreline of the Aleutian Islands. Then, in the early 1990s, the otters started disappearing, and as they disappeared, so did the kelp. The current thinking is that the culprit is a population of "transient" type orca whales that has taken to feeding on otters. The decrease in availability of sea lions and harbor seals as food has forced the whales to turn to less desirable prey. The losers are the otters, the kelp, and all the organisms that prosper in and around the kelp. The only apparent winners are the sea urchins, and possibly some crab species.

Kelp islands

Many seaweeds, like bull kelp and *Macrocystis* (giant kelp), have gas-filled sacs called *pneumatocysts* that float the blades and hold the plant vertical in the water. When separated from their holdfasts these plants float nicely on the sea surface and can travel hundreds of miles with ocean currents and wind. Commercial fishermen often encounter large floating "kelp islands" consisting of tons of plant material, along with driftwood, glass balls, and other flotsam, all wound up in tight knots by tide rips and sailing merrily along for parts unknown. These kelp islands can be refuge and

Top—Kelp floats near shore in the Aleutians. The U.S. Fish and Wildlife Service research vessel, *Tiglax,* is anchored in the distance. Bottom left—A sea otter floats amid bull kelp in the Aleutians. Right—Green sea urchins finish devouring a stand of ribbon kelp at Amchitka Island. Sea otters eat sea urchins, and sea urchins eat kelp. Recently the sea otter population has been shrinking in the Aleutians, allowing sea urchins to flourish. The large sea urchin population has caused destruction of kelp forests which are important habitat for myriad marine species.

feeding areas for many species of fishes and birds.

Kelp harvest

Elsewhere in the world people use kelps for a variety of foods and products, from the delicate black *nori* used to make Japanese sushi, to the industrial applications of *alginates* extracted from seaweeds in paints, medicines, and many processed foods. In the Bering Sea relatively little human use is made of kelps. Native people harvest some herring roe on kelp, usually *Fucus* (rockweed or popweed), and a few people use bull kelp for pickles and ribbon or black kelps in salads or cooked dishes. Some people

> Eelgrass turns what otherwise would be fairly exposed and inhospitable flats into richly productive habitats for a wide range of *infauna* . . . and benthic creatures including crustaceans and small fishes.

A bull whip kelp frond is held up in the current by its buoyant pneumatocyst.

harvest beach cast kelp to use for mulch and fertilizer on their gardens.

Only a single Bering Sea seaweed has achieved commercial status—the humble rockweed. Buyers for Japanese seafood companies each spring buy a few thousand pounds of rockweed covered with herring roe, a product known as *kazunoko kombu*. For a few hours on a couple of tides each season a small army of harvesters combs the rocky shores at places like Togiak Bay, yanking up handfuls of roe-covered rockweed and stuffing it in sacks for delivery to a tender. At the peak of the fishery in the 1980s a harvester could make more than $100 an hour by crawling around on hands and knees ripping kelp from rocks, and the money was a welcome boost in many local house-

holds. But market values have dropped and some years the little fishery doesn't even happen.

Seagrass

Eelgrass (*Zostera*) is not algae, but a flowering plant, that lives in the very shallow water of some tidal inlets and mudflats. Eelgrass turns what otherwise would be fairly exposed and inhospitable flats into richly productive habitats for a wide range of *infauna* (living in the sand or mud) and benthic creatures including crustaceans and small fishes. Many species live out their lives in eelgrass beds, while others rear in them during their larval or juvenile periods and then move to deeper water as adults. Some seabirds and waterfowl, especially geese, eat eelgrass, and route

Top—Izembek Lagoon is located near the town of Cold Bay at the western tip of the Alaska Peninsula. Supporting one of the world's largest eelgrass beds, the lagoon is a major stopover point for migrating birds.
Bottom—A dungeness crab takes cover in eelgrass and a fox looks for food on the eelgrass at Izembek Lagoon.

their migration flights to hit bay after bay where they can fuel up on the slender dark green blades.

Even in death eelgrass is a life-giver; huge windrows of dead *wrack* or eelgrass pile up on beaches to become home and food to many species of amphipods (such as beachhoppers and sea fleas). Many shorebirds benefit from this food resource. Foxes and even bears can sustain themselves during lean times by pawing apart the windrows and gulping thousands of tiny marine organisms.

Life above the Sea
CHAPTER FOUR

T he Bering Sea is home, at least seasonally, to dozens of species of seabirds that live on oceanic waters, plus dozens of shorebirds, waterfowl, raptors (birds of prey), and songbirds that nest along its coastlines. At least 39 species of seabirds have been identified in nesting colonies on the Alaska side alone, and not counted are Asian-only species and another 33 oceanic species that never come ashore in Alaska. Birds range from the tiny 7-inch (18 cm) phalarope to the huge albatross with a seven-foot wingspan (2.3 m). Between 40 million and 50 million seabirds nest each summer on the Bering Sea's shores and islands, about three-fourths of them on the American side. The broad continental shelf, milder winters, and other environmental factors favor the eastern side as bird habitat. At least another 40 million seabirds are nonbreeding seasonal residents. Shearwaters alone number in the tens of millions.

VERENA A. GILL ©

Thick-billed murres and eggs at Bogoslof Island.

Most of the Bering Sea birds go unseen by humans. The few visitors who get to the islands and mainland coasts may observe huge nesting colonies, some with hundreds of thousands of birds hunkered down on tiny ledges brooding their eggs or flying to and from burrows in turf and rock. Nesting lasts only a couple of months each year. The rest of the time most of those birds are far out at sea, riding mountainous, breaking waves in icy winds and darkness, or huddled into polynyas and leads (openings) in the ice. Others are flying thousands of miles over open ocean to wintering grounds off Asia, the Pacific Coast states, or even in the Southern Hemisphere. Those that roost on shore during the winter survive in a land of searing winds, shore ice, and snowdrifts.

Left—Cormorants fly along the Bristol Bay coast.
FRED HIRSCHMANN ©

Between 40 million and 50 million seabirds nest each summer on the Bering Sea's shores and islands, about three-fourths of them on the American side.

Crested auklets are one of the most important bird species harvested as food by subsistence users in the Bering Sea region.

Seabirds

Seabirds differ from other birds in several ways. They are heavier than most birds with layers of fat to retain heat and energy, and drably colored in shades of black and white. Their strategy for reproductive success differs from waterfowl and other birds in that seabirds are long-lived and generally produce only a single egg per year, while other birds lay "clutches" of a half-dozen or more eggs. Kittiwakes and other gulls build neat nests of grass much like upland bird nests, while murres lay their eggs on a bare rock ledge, and puffins and storm-petrels nest underground in burrows. While most have high nesting-site fidelity—that is, they return to the same nest site each year—entire colonies of cormorants may shift nesting locations from one year to the next.

Seabird abundance

Seabird abundance is an indicator of the health of a marine ecosystem, but to gain any understanding from changes in seabird abundance it is necessary to understand how different species fit into the system. For example, a bird that dives is affected by environmental change differently from one that feeds on the surface, and one that winters in the north experiences different stresses from one that migrates to the South Pacific.

Bird abundance can fluctuate because of (1) an increase or decrease in productivity (the success at laying and hatching eggs and raising the young to *fledgling* age when they leave the nest and begin to feed on their own), (2) migration into or out of an area, or (3) changes in the rate of *mortality*, or deaths. Any of these causes can be influenced by changing environmental conditions, but availability of suitable quantities of quality food seems to be what most affects seabird abundance.

Nearly all seabirds eat krill, other zooplankton, or small fish, (including the larval and juvenile forms of larger fish), or some combination of the three. But most birds specialize in specific types of prey and capture strategies and therefore are vulnerable to changes in food availability.

Oceanic birds

In the Bering Sea oceanic birds include some species that do not nest in Alaska and rarely if

Birds, stress, behavior, and survival

The size of some seabird colonies in the Bering Sea has fluctuated a lot during the past few decades. Lack of sufficient food is thought to be a likely reason.

Malnutrition weakens animals and makes them more susceptible to disease. Lack of food also causes stress, and stress triggers the release of stress hormones into the animals' bloodstreams. Prolonged high levels of stress hormones adversely affect an animal's physical vitality. But that's not all. In a laboratory study of kittiwakes, NPMR scientists discovered that excessive stress due to lack of food early in life adversely affects the ability of kittiwakes to learn and remember— their "cognitive" ability.

Kittiwakes rely on their recognition, or cognition, of visual cues in the water to lead them to forage fishes, such as capelin and herring. And so the ability of kittiwakes to learn and remember is critical to their survival.

In the lab, scientists deprived some chicks of adequate food and fed plenty of food to another group.

The researchers did not see much difference in the ability of the chicks in either group to recognize visual cues, such as the color of a food dish, which would lead them to food. However, as the birds grew older, the ones that had been deprived of adequate food

NPMR researchers from the National Park Service and University of Alaska Fairbanks check stress hormone levels in a red-legged kittiwake on Bogolsof Island.

as chicks had a much harder time recognizing and remembering visual cues.

The implication is that kittiwakes that survive to adulthood in the wild after they experience high stress hormone levels as chicks because of an inadequate food supply may not have the brain power later in life to survive as well as birds that get adequate nutrition as chicks.

Arctic tern.

Long-tailed jaegars are common in the upper Bering Sea coastal region.

Nearly 20 gull and kittiwake species occur in Alaska, most of them in the Bering Sea.

ever come ashore. Most are great soarers, traveling long distances by catching air currents to give them lift and propulsion. They spend their time far offshore, with some species preferring the deep ocean waters to the continental shelf.

Most oceanic birds catch small fishes, crustaceans, and squids on or near the surface, while petrels are divers and storm-petrels are surface-plankton eaters. Some can actually smell their prey using specially adapted tubes in their beaks.

Included in this group are three species of albatross, plus the smaller fulmars, shearwaters, petrels, and storm-petrels. Northern fulmars and storm-petrels nest in the region and on nearby islands in the Aleutians and Gulf of Alaska.

Some oceanic seabirds that nest elsewhere spend the northern summers feeding in the Bering Sea. Two species of albatross come up from Hawaii,

and tens of millions of sooty and short-tailed shearwaters arrive from nesting islands in the Southern Hemisphere.

Gulls and terns

Nearly 20 gull and kittiwake species occur in Alaska, most of them in the Bering Sea. Familiar to many are the large gray and white glaucous and glaucous-winged gulls. But other species also occur in the Bering Sea, such as the mew gull, which, at about half the size of the glaucous gull, is the most diminutive of all white-headed gulls.

Other small cousins to the large gulls include two species of kittiwakes, the delicate gulls with the black wing tips as if dipped in ink, seen wheeling over island cliff nesting sites. They eat pollock, sand lance, and some plankton, among other things.

Several species of gulls

Life above the Sea

1. Laysan albatross. 2. Northern fulmar. 3. Black-legged kittiwake and chicks. 4. Fork-tailed storm petrel. 5. Northern fulmars. 6. Aleutian tern. 7. Arctic tern. 8. Mew gull.

Alcids essentially "fly" underwater by flapping their wings as if in the air, and murres are known to dive to nearly 400 feet.

Horned puffins perch on a cliff overlooking the Bering Sea.

are cliff or shore nesters and are surface–fish feeders. Larger gulls eat herring, as well as sand lance and pollock. Some of the bigger gulls are fierce predators and take large numbers of eggs and chicks from the nests of other seabirds.

Most gulls stay in the region throughout the year and spend the winter close to land. The habits of other species are not well known; for example, no one is sure where red-legged kittiwakes spend their winters.

Terns are surface feeders, and shore nesters. Arctic and Aleutian terns nest on sandy and grassy beaches, near either fresh or salt water, and range out to sea to feed on krill. They migrate long distances to their wintering grounds in the Southern Hemisphere.

1. Red-legged kittiwakes congregate on a rock in the Bering Sea. This species breeds exclusively on the Pribilof Islands and on Bogoslof and Buldir islands in the Aleutians. Horned puffins (2) and tufted puffins (3) overlap in range but don't compete for breeding sites because horned puffins nest in rock niches and crevices while tufted puffins generally prefer burrows they dig in steep hillsides and cliffs. 4. Red-faced cormorants are common in the southern Bering Sea. 5. Thick-billed murres loosely tend their eggs on Bogoslof Island in the Aleutians. 6. Parakeet auklets in Alaska are concentrated most heavily in the Bering Sea. 7. A pigeon guillemot holds what appears to be a sand lance. Guillemots fly fast just above the water and suddenly dive in to catch small forage fish.

Snow geese.

Many species of waterfowl, including ducks, geese, and swans occur in the Bering Sea region.

Diving seabirds

Most of the true seabirds are divers, and are capable of descending some distance in search of primarily small fish. Their success is based less on plankton production directly, and more on the availability of forage fishes.

Three species of diving cormorants live in the coastal regions. They are moderately large (wingspan to 34 inches, 86 cm) black diving birds that nest on cliffs. Cormorant colonies can be spotted from miles away by large patches of white guano on the cliffs. Underwater they propel themselves with their feet. They stay in the region year-round and roost on land during the winter.

Alcids are the diving birds most popular with visitors. They include two species of puffins, two species of murres, two species of guillemots, several auklet species, and some murrelets. Most alcids nest either on cliffs or in burrows among the rocks. All alcids winter at sea, with some remaining in the north and others flying as far south as the Hawaiian Islands. Alcids essentially "fly" underwater by flapping their wings as if in the air, and murres are known to dive to nearly 400 feet (133 m). Auklets are plankton feeders while most of the other alcids eat fish.

Non-seabirds

Many of the birds that may be seen on the Bering Sea's waters are not, technically speaking, seabirds. Instead they are in any of several families of birds that nest ashore in reeds, grasses, or tundra and may divide their time between freshwater lakes or rivers and the sea. As such, they may be less influenced by oceanic productivity and more by environmental events on the continent. Still, many derive at least part of their diet, which includes fish, from the sea.

Several species of loons fit into this category, including the brilliantly marked common loon, which is a frequent visitor to coastal waters. Loons are diving birds, as are grebes.

Waterfowl

Many species of waterfowl, including ducks, geese, and swans occur in the Bering Sea region. Alaska has three species of swans but only tundra swans are common along the Bering Sea coast, mainly on ponds. Most of the ducks and geese are primarily freshwater birds, but use the sea and shores at least part of the time. Five species of geese occur along the Bering Sea coast, including the Canada goose with four subspecies, and about 20 species of ducks.

Most of the world's population of black brant (a small goose) flies the eastern shore of the sea and feeds in eelgrass lagoons.

Dabbling ducks feed on or near the surface, commonly on freshwater ponds, and eat grasses and small crustaceans such as beach hoppers and sand fleas. Their feet are located toward the middle of the body, and they leap into the air on takeoff.

Diving ducks have their legs more to the rear end of their bodies and run to get airspeed for takeoff. They use their feet for propulsion under water, and eat primarily invertebrates. Most "sea ducks" are in this group.

USFWS ©

ALISSA CRANDALL©

A. MORRIS/VIREO ©

ALISSA CRANDALL©

ALISSA CRANDALL©

D. ROBY AND K. BRINK/VIREO ©

A. MORRIS/VIREO ©

1. Greater white-fronted goose. 2. Common goldeneyes. 3. American wigeon. 4. Harlequin ducks. 5. Spectacled eiders. 6. Canada goose. 7. Red-necked grebe.

Sea ducks

Sea ducks, including eiders, scoters, and harlequins, are distinct from other waterfowl, in that they winter on the Bering Sea and don't migrate south. Eiders nest on the Arctic tundra of northern Alaska and the Yukon-Kuskokwim Delta but spend their winters where they can find open water on the Bering Sea. These are diving birds that propel themselves underwater with their hind feet, in search of small fishes and invertebrates. Virtually the entire world's population of spectacled eiders has been

Many shorebirds fly long distances to nest and fledge young in the long Bering Sea summer daylight.

A flock of western sandpipers flies over the Bering Sea coast.

found to congregate at a single polynya or opening in the ice, between St. Matthew and St. Lawrence, to spend the winter.

Ducks, geese, swans, and cranes from all over North America, and some from Asia, converge on the freshwater wetlands of the Bering Sea coast, such as the Yukon-Kuskokwim Delta, to feed and nest. Eelgrass beds at places like Izembek Lagoon and Nanvak Bay are major stopover sites for migrating waterfowl.

Shorebirds

Shorebirds comprise a very large group of mostly small and rarely observed Bering Sea birds, although most are migratory and attract notice at other points along their migration paths. Bering Sea shores

are graced by seven species of plovers and 33 species of sandpipers, including phalaropes, snipes, dowitchers, dunlins, stints, turnstones, godwits, whimbrels, curlews, tattlers, and yellowlegs. Kingfishers and sandhill cranes are also part of the coastal bird community.

Many shorebirds fly long distances to nest and fledge young in the long Bering Sea summer daylight. Golden plovers arrive from several distant locations, including southern South America, New Zealand, Australia, and India. Researchers once timed the flight of a bird from Hawaii to King Salmon on Bristol Bay at just 70 hours. Tiny phalaropes winter in the ocean off South America. One species of curlew arrives from islands in the Central Pacific. Several species of very small shorebirds, including

1. Long-billed dowitchers. 2. Dunlin. 3. Short-billed dowitchers. 4. Black-bellied plover. 5. Sandhill cranes. 6. American black oystercatcher. 7. Red-necked phalarope. 8. Semipalmated plover. 9. Western sandpiper. 10. Bristle-thighed curlew.

A rough-legged hawk soars over the Bering Sea.

Many species of songbirds inhabit the region during the summer season and a few upland birds, like ptarmigan, are year-round residents.

A bald eagle feasts on a whale carcass.

sandpipers, yellowlegs, and turnstones, migrate between the Bering Sea and southern South America. The Arctic tern holds the distance record, however, flying from Antarctica to summer on Bering Sea shores.

Hunting birds and songbirds

In addition to water birds, the Bering Sea coast hosts a large number of both seasonal and permanently residing raptors and other hunting birds that find their food in, on, or adjacent to the sea. Most conspicuous are the bald eagle and the less abundant golden eagle. There are numerous falcons,

owls, and hawks as well.

On the Russian side a few additional species occur, including the white-tailed eagle and the huge Steller's sea eagle. A hunting bird with an unusual approach to getting food is the jaeger, which is actually more closely related to gulls than to raptors. They catch small birds and mammals, but their specialty is harassing other birds into dropping or disgorging their food so that the jaeger can scoop it up.

Many species of songbirds inhabit the region during the summer season and a few upland birds, like ptarmigan, are year-round residents. Ravens and magpies also are common.

1. Short-eared owls, common in the Bering Sea region, perch on a crab pot in the Bering Sea. 2. Profile of a northern goshawk, seen mostly in the southern Bering Sea region. 3. A face-on view of a golden eagle, a species less common than bald eagles in the southern Bering Sea. 4. A bald eagle tends its nest. 5. Gyrfalcons, fairly uncommon in the Bering Sea region, feed on other birds and fish. 6. Common in Siberia, this male bluethroat captured along the Bering Sea coast is a rare sight in the U.S. Bering Sea region. 7. A common species in the Bering Sea region, a willow ptarmigan hen and chicks blend in with their surroundings. 8. Golden eagles nest on a cliff top on the Bering Sea coast.

Dobbs Photo

"An interesting Clean up Bessie Bench."

#843

Minerals and Energy
CHAPTER FIVE

H uman use of the Bering Sea has always consisted of extracting and using its living resources. Non-living resources are not well developed. One potential source of great wealth is believed to lie buried far beneath the sands and bedrock of the continental shelf in the form of "fossil fuels."

Formation of hydrocarbon beds

As with its living resources, the story of the Bering Sea's most valuable non-living resources begins with microscopic plankton. Millions of years ago, when the oceans and continents were arranged differently, broad expanses of what is now both undersea and underground was at the earth's surface. Much of it was the seabed of extensive shallow oceans. Millions of generations of microscopic phytoplankton and zooplankton lived out their brief, simple lives in these seas,

The derelict Swanberg gold dredge about one mile outside of Nome.

died, and sank to the bottom. In some cases they were quickly covered by layers of silt and mud, and *aerobic* (in the presence of oxygen) bacterial decomposition didn't have time to occur.

Gradually these areas of sea bottom, covered by hundreds or thousands of feet of sedimentary material, were pushed down by the weight of the sediments deposited on top of them and by forces of continental drift and plate tectonics. They eventually became trapped thousands of feet below the surface by overlying rock. The intense underground pressure and high temperatures

KURT BYERS/UAF ©

Trans-Alaska oil pipeline near Fairbanks.

Vast hydrocarbon deposits are believed to lie under the waters of the continental shelf.

from the earth's core transformed the substance of those tiny plankton cells into *hydrocarbons*. The two most important forms are *crude oil* (petroleum) and *natural gas.*

Coal, formed through compression and heating of vascular plant material like ferns, shrubs, and trees, is deeply buried in the Bering Sea. Coal also is abundant at several locations on the Alaska mainland.

Crude oil and natural gas tend to occur together, and some geological structures have more of one or the other. Oil eventually becomes gas if it is under pressure long enough; therefore the presence of gas may indicate a more thermally mature field.

Extracting oil

Deposits of oil are called *pools* or *reservoirs*, but they are not huge underground caverns of black liquid. The oil is dispersed between and around the grains of sand in the porous and permeable rock that comprises the geological structure of an oil field.

In some reservoirs the oil is under such great pressure, that once the structure is penetrated by drilling the crude will erupt to the surface. In some locations it will flow with mechanical pumping. In other places seawater or natural gas must be re-injected into the field to force the oil out. And in many structures, the oil is there but cannot be extracted by any means currently available.

Oil is used to make motor fuels (gasoline, diesel, and jet fuel), heating fuels, lubricants

(motor oil), solvents, and industrial chemicals. It also can be made into a wide range of petrochemical materials like plastics. Gas can be burned directly as a heating or motor fuel, or it can be processed into any of several liquid fuels through expensive "gas-to-liquid" refining technology. Gas can be liquefied for transport by deeply chilling it and keeping it extremely cold during storage, or it can be shipped directly through gas pipelines in the gaseous state.

Natural gas is a good fuel, but it requires greater investment in processing and transportation and it is much less valuable as it comes out of the ground than crude oil.

America produces domestically about 40 percent of the oil it consumes, a third of which comes from the Gulf of Mexico. The remainder comes from the southern plains, the northern Rocky Mountains, California, and Alaska. Currently Alaska's Cook Inlet and North Slope together produce about a million barrels of crude oil and a billion cubic feet of natural gas daily, but those numbers are decreasing.

Exploration

Vast hydrocarbon deposits are believed to lie under the waters of the continental shelf of the North Slope (including the Beaufort and Chukchi seas), Cook Inlet, and the Bering Sea, including Norton Sound and Bristol Bay. The federal Minerals Management Service (MMS) has designated 14 Alaska OCS (outer continental shelf) planning areas, seven of which are in the Bering Sea, and two others (Hope Basin and Chukchi Sea) are just to the north.

Norton Basin includes Norton Sound and seaward waters to the International Dateline, and includes the Bering Strait area. St. Matthew-Hall lies to the south and includes the waters off the Yukon-Kuskokwim Delta. North Aleutian Basin includes Bristol Bay out to about the longitude of Unimak Pass. Surrounding the Pribilof Islands is the St. George Basin. To the west is Bowers Basin and to the south the Aleutian Basin along the continental slope. Navarin Basin, west of St. Matthew-Hall, lies along the northern edge of the slope and also includes part of the continental shelf.

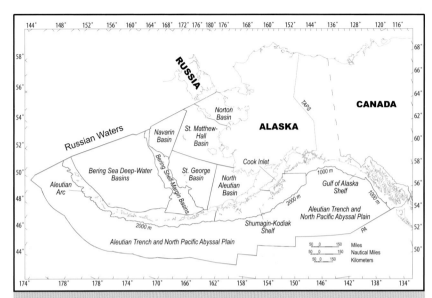

Minerals Management Service has designated 14 Alaska planning areas for exploration, seven of which are in the Bering Sea.

Economics of oil wells

Oil companies don't know where and how much oil may be found, how much is recoverable with existing technology ("conventionally recoverable"), or how much of that can be extracted and sold profitably at current or foreseeable market prices ("economically recoverable"). Tools such as 3-D seismic surveys and geologic modeling can narrow the search, but the only way to find out for sure is to do exploratory drilling. In the last half-century the industry has spent many millions of dollars drilling what turned out to be "dry holes" or finding pools of oil that were not commercially viable to develop.

MMS estimates that 87 percent of the 24.86 billion barrels of conventionally recoverable oil is not economically recoverable under current market conditions, based on an average price of $18 per barrel. Of the economically recoverable 3.26 billion barrels about 85 percent is located beneath the Chukchi and Beaufort seas, adjacent to the oil-producing area of the North Slope. While the government estimates that 30 million barrels of oil lie below the Bering Shelf, little is recoverable under current market projections, and industry has shown little interest in the region. A proposed Navarin Basin sale in the Bering Sea was cancelled because oil companies did not express intent to bid. It appears that no OCS oil drilling is likely in the first decade of the twenty-first century.

Natural gas production

The natural gas situation is similar. MMS estimates the state's natural gas production potential is 122.58 trillion cubic feet, which corresponds to the 24.86 billion barrels of conventionally recoverable oil. Only four percent of that, however, is economically recoverable, and 69 percent of the economically recoverable four percent is in the Arctic. The Bering Shelf is estimated to hold 990 billion cubic feet of gas, which is not attracting industry interest.

How much oil and gas?

Five of the Bering Shelf subregion's seven areas are believed to have conventionally recoverable reserves: Navarin Basin, North Aleutian Basin, St. George Basin, Norton Basin, and St. Matthew-Hall. As much as two billion barrels of oil and 54 billion cubic feet of natural gas may lie beneath the waves.

In the late 1970s and early 1980s exploration companies

Deposits that lie under the icy waves are believed to be primarily natural gas.

drilled several COST (continental offshore stratigraphic test) wells in St. George, Norton Sound, Navarin Basin, and North Aleutian Basin. Lease sales were held in the mid-1980s and almost two million acres (8,100 sq km) were awarded. Companies drilled two dozen exploratory wells but none produced significant amounts of oil or gas.

The industry felt its best chance for success was in the North Aleutian Basin, at the outer edge of Bristol Bay. In 1988 oil companies purchased 23 leases in the area, but commercial fishermen and the state government protested. They were concerned about damage that oil drilling and oil spills might do to the tremendously valuable salmon and herring fisheries. In 1989 Congress passed—and in 1990 MMS implemented—a one-year drilling moratorium, which was extended one year at a time and is in effect until 2012. The companies relinquished their leases in 1995 when the federal government agreed to buy them back.

Bering Sea leasing

In the five-year leasing program starting in 2003, MMS is offering part of Norton Sound for lease as a "special interest sale." MMS believes that the oil and/or gas are not commercially viable in the world market. The area includes about 25 million acres (101,000 sq km) of the continental shelf, located from three to 320 miles offshore (5-520 km) to the south and west of the Seward Peninsula.

MMS has no additional plans for oil and gas leasing in the Bering Sea until 2008. However, the State of Alaska plans to offer tracts onshore and in nearshore waters of Bristol Bay for oil and gas drilling. State-owned resources could support a hydrocarbon industry there if industry commits to exploration.

On the Russian side

Meanwhile, exploratory drilling is occurring on the Russian side, off the Chukotka coast in the Gulf of Anadyr. Little information is available about Russian hydrocarbon prospecting in the Bering Sea, but at this time the drilling is exploratory and no production has begun.

Threat of oil pollution?

While the Bering Sea itself is not likely to see drilling soon, the hydrocarbon industry could still have an effect on it. If the Chukchi Sea and Hope Basin are explored in the future, the Bering Sea will be a transportation corridor for petroleum-related industrial equipment and supplies, and could be affected by a spill.

Both Russian and American interests are studying the prospects of transporting oil out of the Arctic by conventional tanker ship, or possibly by submarine. These ships would pass through the Bering Sea, and carry with them the threat of massive oil spills should an accident occur. Also, oil spilled at interior continental sites adjacent to tributary rivers could bring unwanted hydrocarbons to the basin. Currently and for the foreseeable future, Alaska oil development activity is in river drainages that do not flow into the Bering Sea. So far it appears that in Russia, too, the areas under active development drain to the Pacific Ocean, the Sea of Okhotsk, and Arctic Ocean, not into the Bering Sea.

Gas hydrates

Another form of fossil hydrocarbon energy may someday come under development in the Bering Sea. Scientists in the Canadian Arctic now are exploring reserves of gas hydrate, a form of solidified natural gas that is believed to occur in vast quantities across the Arctic and parts of the sub-Arctic, including at several locations beneath the Bering Sea.

Gas hydrate is a solid that looks like ice and is made of methane (natural gas) locked into a lattice structure of frozen water molecules. It is formed under conditions of high pressure and very cold temperatures, and extraction is difficult. Deposits of gas hydrate are not thick enough to warrant mining, and it will not flow from the ground unless warmed by hot water or some other heat source. It is believed that huge hydrate deposits exist worldwide—enough to supply the world's energy needs for centuries, if they could be economically extracted and converted into usable fuels. Today the

Top—Massive container ships, like this one at Kodiak shown taking on freezer vans full of fish and crab, ply the North Pacific. Bottom—The U.S. Coast Guard cutter *Alex Haley* tows a cargo ship that lost power in the Bering Sea.

Shipping industry

Hundreds of large container ships transit the Bering Sea via Unimak Pass every year, carrying goods traded between Asia and North America—cars, electronics, clothing, etc.

These ships are making the "great circle" between the west coast of North America and Asia. The great circle takes them north of the Aleutians because the route is shorter than crossing the Pacific. Thus, the Bering Sea is an important international economic resource as part of an intercontinental transportation corridor.

Each ship carries hundreds of thousands of gallons of its own heavy fuel oil, so transit of these big vessels brings with it the risk of serious environmental damage if one of these ships should break up or go aground.

Steadman Avenue in Nome, 1900.

In the late 1890s Nome emerged as the center of a gold rush on the north shore of Norton Sound.

technology to do this does not exist.

Scientists have identified several structures under the Bering Sea believed to contain gas hydrate, most of them in the deep basin on the Russian side. The technical challenges combined with the problems of economic viability suggest that any exploitation of Bering Sea gas hydrate resources is in the distant future, if at all. Still, it is a resource that some scientists and technologists will turn their attention to if and when market conditions change.

Mining gold

In the late 1890s Nome emerged as the center of a gold rush on the north shore of Norton Sound. Some small-scale suction dredging and placer mining operations continue to operate on Nome-area beaches and on subtidal

bottom within the 3-mile (4.9 km) state territorial waters. MMS offered gold leases in federal waters in the late 1980s but got no bids.

Gold and platinum are known to occur farther south near Goodnews Bay, but no offshore leasing is currently being considered.

Occasionally there has been interest in mining sand and gravel from the seafloor for use in local construction and village relocation projects, but no specific plans have been made. Rock is transported to and from several coastal villages in the Bering Sea, although most of it is mined at onshore locations.

Small dredges like this one at Nome are used to vacuum up bottom sediments near the shore, from which gold particles are extracted.

Minerals and Energy

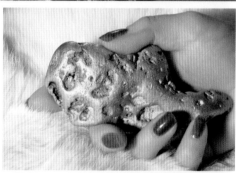

1. Known as the Last Train to Nowhere, derelict steam engines and rolling stock lie sinking into the tundra near Nome. After four years of construction, only 35 miles of track were laid, and the project was abandoned in 1907. 2. This is what a 24 oz gold nugget looks like, taken from a small mine in Interior Alaska. 3. One of several old gold dredges, this one about 6 miles from Nome. 4. A hydraulic lift near Nome sucks up soil and gravel that contain gold, circa 1900.

Minerals and Energy

Happy Jack the Ivory Carver
and Family
Nome Alaska.

H.G.Kaiser
Photo

Culture and Commerce
CHAPTER SIX

T he Bering Sea wasn't always what it is today. In fact, it wasn't always a sea. During several long periods of pre-history much of it was a broad plain, something like a tundra or savanna. During the last ice age, 12,000-15,000 years ago, so much of the earth's water was locked up in glaciers that sea level fell 300 feet (100 m), again exposing a thousand-mile-wide (1,600 km) expanse of fertile lowland. It was inhabited by a rich array of vegetation and animals; mastodons were there, and saber-tooth cats, and brown bears probably were too. During part of the time an earlier and smaller version of the Yukon River meandered down from the highlands of central Alaska and made a broad arc to flow into the Arctic.

Scientists believe that the first wave of people to see North America, over a series of generations crossed the wide plain called the Bering Land Bridge, and arrived in Alaska even earlier than the last ice

age, perhaps as early as 30,000 years ago. Probably they followed migrating game animals across the plain. They may have found the slightly milder climate and more productive lands on the North American side to their liking. Once established on this side, people spread across the continent and eventually

throughout the Americas. They were ancestors to American Indians.

A subsequent wave, which included distant ancestors of today's Eskimos and Aleuts, crossed over 9,000 years ago (or more recently) and settled on the shores of the Bering Sea and across northern Alaska. The land bridge was a corridor not

Left—A Yupik family in Nome.
KAVIK HAHN COLLECTION, UAF ALASKA AND POLAR REGIONS DEPARTMENT ©

Above—Ice age mammals of Alaska.
ILLUSTRATION BY JAY H. MATTERNES © 1972. PHOTO BY KURT BYERS

KURT BYERS/ UAF ©

A Yupik elder at Hooper Bay.

The indigenous people who now inhabit the north are probably not direct descendants of the original immigrants, but rather of more recent arrivals who displaced them.

only for people but also for plants, mammals, birds, and probably even some freshwater fishes. It is striking that about two-thirds of the species of plants and animals are exactly the same on both sides of the Bering Sea, while the rest are totally different. It is believed that the migration of humans was east from Asia to America, but that may not be true of all species. Some plants, mammals, birds, and fishes likely migrated west into Asia from North America.

Eventually the climate warmed, the polar ice caps and continental glaciers melted, the sea level rose, and a wide, relatively shallow sea filled in the space. While it may be comforting to think that this is a permanent state, scientists tell us that the sea probably will rise even higher, and yet another ice age someday will shrink it back down.

By about 100,000 years ago people of the modern human race had migrated from Africa across the world, and by 12,000 years ago people had entered the New World. The groups who crossed into North America spread across the continent. Over many generations they eventually worked their way south until they halted at land's end at Tierra del Fuego, the southern tip of South America.

The timing, direction, and purpose of all this migration is to some extent theory. Archeologists and anthropologists have several ideas about who went where and when. Following is a summary of what archeological evidence suggests.

Origins of Alaska Native people

There was not a single human migration, but several. The indigenous people who currently inhabit the north are probably not direct descendants of the original immigrants, but rather of more recent arrivals who displaced them. It is believed that earliest arrivals crossed the northern part of the land bridge, near the Bering Strait. Over time their descendants migrated south to become the Indians of North, Central, and South America. Later immigrants were the ancestors of Aleut and Eskimo peoples. Some went southwest and gave rise to the Aleuts, while others fanned out across the northern extremes of the continent, as far east as Greenland, and were ancestors to Eskimos.

While "Eskimo" is not a term most people of that heritage use to describe themselves, it is useful for describing several groups in Alaska. In Canada where all the "Eskimo" people are of the Inuit group, the term Eskimo is not used.

Yupiks and Inupiat

On the North America side of the Bering Sea are two major Eskimo language groups, Yupik and Inuit, with several dialects and cultures. People of the major southern group inhabit the Alaska coast from Bristol Bay to northern Norton Sound, and they call themselves Yupik. The northern

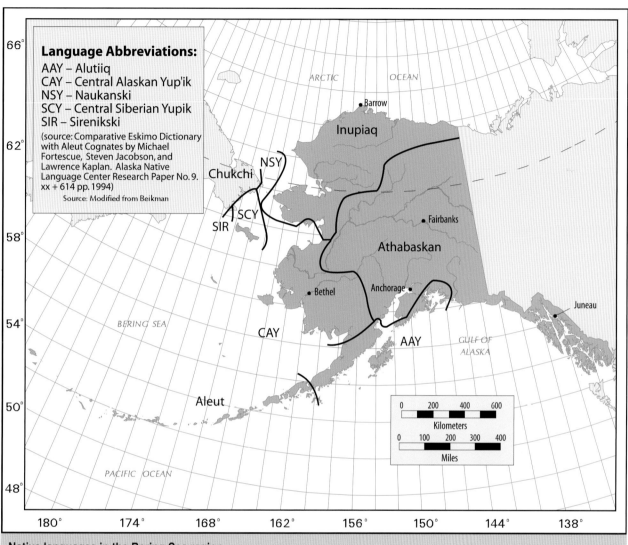

Language Abbreviations:

AAY – Alutiiq
CAY – Central Alaskan Yup'ik
NSY – Naukanski
SCY – Central Siberian Yupik
SIR – Sirenikski

(source: Comparative Eskimo Dictionary with Aleut Cognates by Michael Fortescue, Steven Jacobson, and Lawrence Kaplan. Alaska Native Language Center Research Paper No. 9. xx + 614 pp. 1994)

Source: Modified from Beikman

Native languages in the Bering Sea region.

Inuit group ranges from the Seward Peninsula (some overlap with Yupiks), past the Bering Strait, along the coast of the Chukchi and Beaufort seas, all the way to Greenland. In Alaska the Inuit people are called Inupiaq (plural Inupiat).

The Yupiks and Inupiat share many characteristics of diet, material culture, and oral tradition, but have distinct cultures and languages. The Yupik branch of Eskimo includes four languages. Alutiiq (also known as Sugpiaq) is on the Alaska Peninsula, Kodiak Island, the tip of the Kenai Peninsula, and Prince William Sound. Central Yup'ik (with an apostrophe), is spoken in Southwestern Alaska around Bristol Bay and on the Yukon-Kuskokwim Delta. Naukan Yupik is spoken only on the Russian side across from the Diomedes. And Siberian Yupik is spoken on St. Lawrence Island and across the strait on the Russian side. In the area of Nelson Island and Nunivak Island, the people of several villages speak Cup'ik, a dialect of Central Yup'ik.

While predominantly coastal peoples, both Yupik and Inupiaq communities exist far inland, particularly on the major rivers. The Yupik village of Koliganek is 80 miles (140 km) up the Nushagak River, and on the Kuskokwim and Yukon river villages predominantly of Yupik people are more than

Based on language and cultural traditions Alutiiq are considered by anthropologists to be directly related to Yupik people.

This watercolor painting created by Mikhail Tikhanov in 1818 depicts Alutiiq men from Kodiak demonstrating use of a bow-and-arrow and a spear. Both wear spruce root hats.

100 miles upriver (160 km).

The Alutiiq people inhabit southern Bristol Bay, parts of the Alaska Peninsula, and southern Cook Inlet. Two hundred years of shared history beginning with the arrival of the Russians, and a similar lifestyle, have resulted in some Alutiiq calling themselves "Aleut." But they do not have the same origins as the Aleuts described below. Based on language and cultural traditions Alutiiq are considered by anthropologists to be directly related to Yupik people.

Aleuts

Aleuts are the people of the Aleutian, Pribilof, and Shumagin islands and western Alaska

Peninsula. It is believed that a group of people migrated across the southern part of the land bridge to an area near what is now Umnak Island in the eastern Aleutians, which at that time was the west end of the Alaska Peninsula. About 9,000 years ago, or more recently, part of that migration moved north and became Eskimos, while others spread out west and east along the Aleutian chain and the Alaska Peninsula to become Aleuts. Their language is different from the other Alaska Eskimo languages.

All subgroups of Eskimo people are distinct from American Indians, not only in language and culture but also in physical characteristics.

Children mug for the camera in Hooper Bay, a Yupik village on the Bering Sea coast. Despite high teacher salaries, villages have trouble retaining teachers due to the demanding living conditions and high cost of living.

Impacts on indigenous peoples

Native people of Alaska's Bering Sea coast inhabit more than 100 communities, most of them remote small villages located near productive fishing and hunting sites and a source of fresh water. Many of these villagers have retained much of their language and culture. However, the arrival of non-Natives more than 200 years ago resulted in a great deal of genetic and cultural mixing over the centuries. First Russian fur traders, then Yankee whalers and sealers contributed their genes to the pool.

More recently prospectors, commercial fishermen, cannery workers, teachers, and civil servants have contributed to the rich cultural mix. Some Bering Sea Native people can trace their family line to Japanese,

Filipino, Norwegian, German, Scottish, or Yugoslav antecedents.

Irrespective of where the majority of a person's ancestors came from he or she needed only one Native grandparent to qualify for Native status under the Alaska Native Claims Settlement Act. For other purposes any Native ancestry is sufficient, and in many cases the determinant of Native status is tribal enrollment. The tribes themselves determine whom to include as members.

Historically, indigenous groups feuded and warred with one another. In fact, bloody conflicts were fought between the nations and among tribes, with raiding between villages. In most cases the fighting was to protect prime harvesting sites or boundaries that divided territories. Sometimes the dividing line was a river or the crest of a mountain range, and those features remain real boundaries

that delineate Native political and economic divisions even today.

Starting with the advent of Christian missionaries with their churches and schools, the animosities between Native groups began to dissolve. Statehood, the Alaska Native Claims Settlement Act, new laws pertaining to provision of public education, the development of school athletic programs, and a myriad of other changes to the cultural landscape, have brought the peoples of the coast and all of Alaska together under the single title of Alaska Native. Individuals intermarry, are welcomed into one another's villages, and participate in social and economic activities that unite previously hostile communities. To be sure, vestiges of discrimination and intercultural animosity remain, but in general the communities of Western Alaska are fully integrated and the territorial wars are now a part of history.

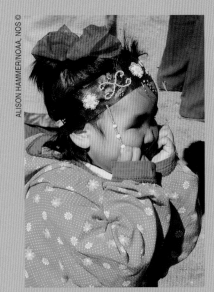

A Native child at Lorino, Russia.

Murders and coordinated attacks on Native communities took their toll, but disease killed far more people.

Russian Natives

Over in the Russian Far East the Native culture picture is even more complex. The Ainu people in Japan once lived on southern Kamchatka. With the coming of Russians they were displaced first to the Kuril Islands and Sakhalin, and now live only on Hokkaido. Another group, known as Kamchadal, now reside on southern Kamchatka. Kamchadal are a mix of Russian and a Native group of the peninsula, Itel'man. Other peoples live on the peninsula and on the lands to the north—Even and Koryak, who are reindeer herders, and Evenk, Yupik, and Chukchi, who in part get subsistence from the sea. As in Alaska, a great deal of racial and cultural mixing has occurred in the last two and a half centuries, but the sheer remoteness and lack of transportation and commerce on the Russian side has allowed greater fidelity to ancient traditions.

Russians bring changes

Native peoples pretty much had the Bering Sea to themselves until 1648 when a Russian ship under the command of an officer by the name of Dezhnev sailed through the Bering Strait from the Arctic. In 1728 Danish captain Vitus Bering, in the service of the Russian navy, explored the western shores of the Bering Sea and named St. Lawrence and the Diomede islands. Bering returned in

1741, but was shipwrecked on the stormy coast of the Kommandor Islands.

Fur trade

Bering himself didn't survive the voyage. Those of his expedition who did survive returned to Petropavlovsk with 900 sea otter pelts and reports of abundant sea otters and fur seals in Alaska. The luxurious pelt of the sea otter was one of the most valuable commodities from northern waters, and soon heavily armed *promuishlenniki* (hunters or traders) stormed the remote shores, bringing destruction to the Aleut people and sea otters alike.

Tragedy for Aleuts

By the middle of the 1700s the first economic boom was on. While it made some Russians rich, it was for the most part a tragedy for the Aleuts. Had the Russians simply hunted and purchased pelts, it may not have been so bad. But their approach was to wage war on the Native people, killing many, displacing the rest from their homes, and enslaving able-bodied hunters to do their work for them. In the early decades of Russian trading the mix of independent trading companies, commercial and personal rivalries, and distance from authority made the Alaska frontier a lawless place. Murders and coordinated attacks on Native communities took their toll, but disease killed far more people. Up to 80 percent of the Aleuts died in the early years of contact, most from disease. By the late 1700s Aleut men were held in

KAMTCHATKA.
Chasse aux Macareux.

Des: d'ap: nat: par H. Kittlitz. *Imp: lith: d'Engelmann & Cᵉ à Paris.* *Lith par Sabatier Fig: par V. Adam.*

Naturalist Friedrich von Kittlitz created this lithograph in 1835, which depicts him and companions in 1826 or 1827 collecting puffins and puffin eggs for food near Petropavlovsk on the Kamchatka Peninsula. The Kittlitz's murrelet bears his name. Other naturalists likewise were immortalized. For example, the Steller sea lion, Steller's eider, and Steller's sea cow are named after Georg Wilhelm Steller, who accompanied Vitus Bering on one of his expeditions.

servitude to hunt sea otters and fur seals for the Russian traders. Entire villages were relocated for the convenience of the invaders, sometimes to distant points on the Alaska coast.

In 1787 Gerassin Pribilov moved 137 Aleuts from Atka and Unalaska to St. Paul Island to hunt fur seals. This was the start of human habitation in the Pribilof Islands. Other Aleuts were relocated to the Sitka area of Southeast Alaska, and to the Kommandor Islands, where a few hundred still live today. Many Aleuts died during long sea voyages by kayak under Russian control. And more than 100 died in a single night at a place now called Poison Cove, off Peril Strait near Sitka, from eating mussels contaminated by naturally occurring paralytic shellfish poisoning.

Violence lessens

Sea otter hunting peaked during the period 1760-1780. In 1799 Czar Paul I granted an exclusive charter to the Russian American Company to conduct trade in the colony. After that date, violence toward the original inhabitants largely diminished, although substantial damage had already been done to Alaska Native cultures. Competing traders and hunters returned to Russia or became company employees and were required to uphold company standards. Russians could come to Alaska only with a work

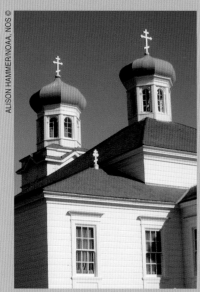

ALISON HAMMER/NOAA, NOS ©

Church of the Holy Ascension, Dutch Harbor.

Today many Alaska Native people have Russian names, as do many islands, bays, mountains, straits, and other geographical features.

contract, and the total population ranged from about 400 to 800 people at any given time during the 132-year period of Russian occupation.

Under the Russian American Company administration, most Aleuts were company employees and had a somewhat higher status than serfs in Russia. The Aleuts of the Near Islands (the westernmost group of islands in the Aleutian chain) were not company employees but maintained economic and political independence through the period of Russian occupation. But all Native people were considered citizens of the Russian empire. After the United States took control of Alaska, Natives had to wait more than 50 years for U.S. citizenship.

Religion and education

Along with commerce, the Russians also brought religion and education. The first Russian Orthodox priests arrived in 1795, and within a few decades, tiny wooden onion dome–topped Russian Orthodox churches sprouted up along the coast, from St. Michael in the north, to the far western Aleutians, to Sitka and Wrangell in Southeast Alaska and as far south as Fort Ross in northern California. For many people the Orthodox cross came to symbolize civilization and enlightenment. Priests developed alphabets for Native languages and taught people to read and write. Young Natives and people of mixed race parentage became bilingual and partici-

pated in the cultural, intellectual, and commercial life of the colony. The clergy taught construction and agricultural skills. Native people took to the strange foreign religion, which gradually displaced their own spiritualism.

Russians married Native women, and priests conveyed Russian names on their parishioners and on the landscape around them. Today many Alaska Native people have Russian names, as do many islands, bays, mountains, straits, and other geographical features. Nikolski, St. Paul, St. George, Golovin, and Cape Romanzof are Bering Sea villages whose names reveal their Russian origins. The Russian Orthodox Church has survived the cataclysmic changes that occurred in Alaska during the last two and a half centuries, and has even prospered.

British, Spanish, and French arrive

As sea mammal stocks diminished and fur markets changed, hunters affiliated with the Russian American Company turned their attention to terrestrial animals and continued their trade. In 1821 Czar Alexander I issued a declaration which claimed Russian sovereignty over all of the Alaska coast as far north as the Bering Strait, prohibiting foreign vessels from fishing, whaling, and trading there. But worrisome incursions by British vessels, encroachment by Britain's Hudson's Bay Company, and expensive wars closer to home eventually convinced the czar that Alaska was more of a liability than an asset.

British captain James Cook had explored the Gulf of Alaska coast and the Bering Sea as early as 1778, and Spanish expeditions launched from Baja California reached the Aleutians. French vessels explored the Gulf of Alaska coast. The Russian court feared loss of commercial influence in the area to aggressive foreigners. Furthermore, Russia's defeat by British and French forces in the Crimean War in 1856 left the Russians leery of entanglements in distant and hard-to-defend locations.

Sale of Alaska to United States

In 1867 Secretary of State William Seward, in a series of closed-door negotiations worthy of present-day politicians, struck a deal with his Russian counterpart to purchase the entire colony for $7.2 million. Seward was ridiculed in the press for his actions, and Congress refused to pay for its purchase for more than a year, but Seward is now considered a hero for his vision of the future.

The purchase treaty was supposed to preserve the rights of Russian residents in Alaska, but Americanization began almost immediately and most returned to Russia in short order. Native people fared a little better. The treaty acknowledged land claims and certain rights to cultural and linguistic identity, but an informal program to exterminate Native languages was fairly successful. Thanks

to efforts of the Russian Orthodox church and others, many indigenous languages survived.

Russians return in 1900s

While the original stock of Russians who came as fur buyers departed or died out after the American purchase of Alaska, at least two subsequent waves of Russians have arrived on these shores. In the 1960s a small group of *Staroveri* ("Old Believers"), whose ancestors had fled religious persecution in nineteenth century Russia, began arriving from Oregon and established several villages on the southern Kenai Peninsula and near Kodiak. They have been major participants in the Bristol Bay salmon and Aleutian longline fisheries. More recently, with the dissolution of the Soviet Union many people have immigrated from Russia to Alaska, where they have become teachers, scientists,

Top—A Russian Orthodox church retains its traditional splendor at St. Paul in the Pribilof Islands. Bottom—A Russian Orthodox cemetery at Dutch Harbor honors the memory of past generations.

professionals, and, of course, fishermen.

Christian missionaries

The Russian Orthodox church was the first to bring Christianity to western Alaska's Native people, but not the last. Both Catholic and Moravian missionaries arrived after the American purchase of Alaska. The U.S.

An umiak boat skeleton and rack frames St. Joseph's Catholic church in Nome.

People on the Bering Sea coast are among the poorest people in the nation in terms of per capita income, health, high school test scores, and other conventional measurements.

government divided the territory among the competing faiths. Every village had one of the three main denominations, and a few had more than one. The Catholic and Moravian missionaries felt free to convert Russian Orthodox practitioners to their beliefs.

In more recent years evangelicals and mainstream Christian denominations have established a foothold in most villages. The larger towns now have the three original churches plus a number of newer arrivals. In Bristol Bay there is a large Seventh Day Adventist community. The village of Aleknagik became an Adventist haven for Yupik people fleeing what they perceived as the moral decay of their home villages. Today tolerance and brotherhood prevail among the various Christian sects in the region, but other religions still are scarce to nonexistent.

Economic status

Alaska's Native people have both flourished and suffered under the Western occupation that continues to this day. Health services have lengthened life spans and reduced infant mortality. The cash economy brought technologies that have made village life far easier, more comfortable, and more interesting. For some, exciting career opportunities have opened up and participation in the wider world has become possible.

But historically Native people have had lower-paying jobs than non-Natives, if any jobs at all, while enduring the highest cost of living of any people in the United States. People on the Bering Sea coast are among the poorest people in the nation in terms of per capita income, health, high school test scores, and other conventional measurements. While the 1971 Alaska Native Claims Settlement Act (ANCSA) conveyed valuable assets in the form of timber lands and oil-bearing properties to 13 Native Regional Corporations, the Bering Sea people got little of value. They have entitlement to huge tracts of land but most of it has little revenue-producing capability.

The cash economy of the region north of Bristol Bay is based on a low value commercial fishery and a small amount of tourism, but primarily on government services and financial assistance. The Bristol Bay fishery historically has better provided for the people of that region. Many Arctic-Yukon-Kuskokwim residents migrate south to fish the bay in season, but changes in market conditions and the effects of climate on fish runs are depressing the value of even that salmon fishery. Arctic-Yukon-Kuskokwim (AYK) includes Norton Sound and Kotzebue Sound.

Hooper Bay (all above) is a relatively large Yupik Eskimo Native village with 1,000 residents on the Yukon-Kuskokwim Delta. In 2000, approximately 28 percent of the households were under the U.S. poverty level. Employment is mostly in the seasonal commercial fishing industry. Most Western Alaska villages do not have indoor plumbing because the cost is too high. In Hooper Bay, residents get well water from central "washaterias," and take their domestic liquid waste to portable receptacles, called "honey buckets" (bottom right). The honey buckets are periodically hauled away and dumped into specially designated lagoons. In some villages, some dwellings are equipped with domestic liquid waste holding tanks. Pump trucks come by, pump out the tanks, and transport the waste to lagoons. Hooper Bay's 400-student school has its own water system. In 2003, construction was under way on a better water system for the rest of the village.

Blackfish drying at
Kalskag.

Young people
in Chukotka are
learning nearly
forgotten marine
mammal hunting
skills, not to main-
tain their cultural
identity, but
simply to feed
their families.

Subsistence as a way of life

Cash is scarce but the region is wealthy in subsistence resources. Salmon, herring, halibut, cod, smelt, trout, Dolly Varden and Arctic char, pike, whitefish, sheefish, and blackfish are harvested intensively for food. Seals, sea lions, walruses, bowhead and belukha whales, and seabirds and their eggs make up a significant part of the diets of Bering Sea coastal residents, as do caribou and moose in some locations, reindeer and muskoxen in others, as well as porcupine, beaver, muskrat, and hare. Native people pick copious volumes of berries, with entire families taking to the hillsides to harvest the bounty. They also eat roots, bulbs, and leaves of plants on the shore and inland. People even collect the bulbs of wild plants that have been stored in underground caches by field mice; it's called "mouse food" and is a delicacy because the rodents have already peeled and cleaned the bulbs.

It is difficult for urbanites to understand the importance of subsistence to village dwellers. Per capita consumption of subsistence foods in Bering Sea villages ranges from 300 to 600 pounds per year (140-280 kg). With incomes less than half the statewide average and food prices double, household economies depend heavily on locally harvested wild foods. And the significance goes far beyond the financial value of the food obtained. Whereas

Boys in Savoonga practice cleaning seal hides in a special program designed to maintain traditional subsistence practices.

Living off the land is still a way of life in Western Alaska. 1. A rancher herds reindeer in a corral near Nome. 2. A Native boy shows off some murre eggs. 3. A trapper at Naknek skins a mink while a fox skin dries in the foreground. 4. Salmon and laundry dry together outside a home at Akutan. 5. Kids enjoy grilled reindeer at a Fourth of July barbecue at St. Paul. 6. A Nome resident picks a plant to use for medicinal purposes. 7. A woman does some ice fishing on Little Diomede Island.

A marine mammal bone pile at Savoonga.

Caribou, a close relative to reindeer, are a staple in many Native Alaskans' diets.

Subsistence, if anything, is even more vital to Native people on the Russian side because of the poor state of the post-Soviet regional economy.

other Americans may achieve personal identity and satisfaction from career, acquisition, recreation, and religion, rural Native people achieve the same in part through skills related to hunting and fishing, food preservation and preparation, and cultural values associated with sharing within the community and providing for the needs of relatives and neighbors.

Many Native people allude to a spiritual component of their subsistence activities. Others claim that only subsistence foods provide them the nutrition they need to maintain their health. Regional Native health corporations have come to recognize the value of subsistence foods and are finding ways to provide these types of foods to Natives in hospitals

and long-term care units.

Even in the larger population centers, like Dillingham and Nome, where in the evening living rooms of houses are lit by the eerie glow of CNN or the Internet on the computer screen, hunters still tow the walrus and belukha whale to the beach where their neighbors butcher the animals and share the meat with the community. Drying racks and smokehouses are ubiquitous in the residential neighborhoods of these towns.

Politics of subsistence

Subsistence has become a major political football in Alaska, as the balance of legislative power has gradually but firmly shifted from rural ("bush") to urban politicians. Under the federal Alaska National Interest Lands Conservation Act (ANILCA), priority in allocation of fish and game resources on federal lands (which is most of Alaska) goes to rural residents. Years of litigation and political wrangling have gone into the precise legal definition of "rural." In the end all efforts were for naught. The Alaska Supreme Court determined that the federal law contradicts the state constitution, which guarantees equal access to all.

For the most part the subsistence issue is a hypothetical conflict, since priority applies only in times of shortage, and rarely has a shortage of fish or game been a real factor in Alaska. But a growing urban and suburban population is demanding more fish and game for recreation, and the possibility of shortages now exists.

Because Alaska law is out of compliance with ANILCA the federal government has taken control of fish and game management on federal lands. The only way the state could regain management authority would be for the people to amend the state constitution, removing the equal access provision and allowing for a rural subsistence preference. Urban state legislators, backed by a hard-core contingent of urban sport hunters, have stymied all attempts at putting up a subsistence constitutional amendment for a vote of the public. The consequence may be far-reaching and could bring about additional restrictions on sport and commercial fishing as federal managers try to control

Residents of Yanrakino, Russia, tend to their daily business.

activities that could diminish the amount of fish available to subsistence users.

Russian Natives

Subsistence, if anything, is even more vital to Native people on the Russian side because of the poor state of the post-Soviet regional economy. Mainstays of the region—reindeer herding, fur farming, commercial sea mammal hunting, and Soviet financial assistance—have ceased. Freighters no longer stop to deliver fuel and supplies at some villages, and without fuel power plants no longer produce heat and electricity. The population has decreased because people who had money for a ticket out have left, and among those remaining the mortality rate has increased. In contrast, some Kamchatka villages have actually seen a population increase as residents produce more infants for the $15 monthly

Harpoon points in whale bone.

Commercial harvests depleted the stocks but the cessation of American walrus hunting came in time and the stocks recovered.

support provided by the government. Young people in Chukotka are learning nearly forgotten marine mammal hunting skills, not to maintain their cultural identity but to feed their families.

Commercial harvest of mammals

In 1867, when the United States bought the American shore of the Bering Sea along with all of Alaska from Russia, in a sort of going-out-of-business sale, commerce not only was established but already was in the first stages of transformation. Sea otters had been hunted down to a point where their pursuit was unprofitable.

Whale harvest

Starting in the 1840s Yankee whalers began hunting in the Bering, Chukchi, and Beaufort seas, taking humpbacks, rights, grays, sperms, bowheads, and minkes. The peak of whaling during the mid-nineteenth century lasted only a few decades, but whaling continued on a much-diminished scale into the 1970s, with Dutch Harbor one of the last operating whaling ports in the country.

Walrus harvest

When the whales got scarce in the late 1800s, whalers switched to hunting walruses. Walruses were taken for their oil (similar to whale oil), hides (used for drive belts and sharpening strops), and tusks (similar to elephant ivory). In the last decades of the 1800s commercial hunters killed some 200,000 walruses, severely depleting the stock. The American commercial hunt nearly ceased in the 1920s due to the shortage of walruses, and was prohibited by law in 1941. Soon after that the walrus stocks began to rebuild, and

THE WHALE FISHERY.
Aleuts planting glass, obsidian, and jade darts in a school of humpback whales, Akoon Island, Bering Sea. (Sect. v, vol. ii, pp. 61, 62.)
Drawing by H. W. Elliott.

Natives pursue two humpback whales in this 1883 illustration of a whale hunt at Akun Island in the Bering Sea.

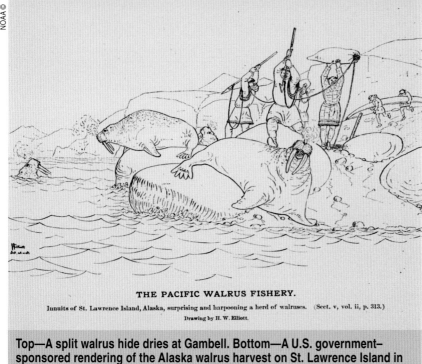

THE PACIFIC WALRUS FISHERY.

Innuits of St. Lawrence Island, Alaska, surprising and harpooning a herd of walruses. (Sect. v, vol. ii, p. 313.)

Drawing by H. W. Elliott.

Top—A split walrus hide dries at Gambell. Bottom—A U.S. government–sponsored rendering of the Alaska walrus harvest on St. Lawrence Island in 1883.

are believed to be well within the limits to preserve a sustainable walrus population. The Eskimo Walrus Commission, representing Western Alaska Natives, along with the U.S. Fish and Wildlife Service, have developed an international agreement with Russia on walrus management, and a similar agreement exists for polar bears.

Seal harvest

Long before the commercial whale and walrus industries had died out, focus had shifted to the enormous numbers of fur seals, which drew fleets from the United States, Canada, and Japan. Pelts of the fur seal are much richer than those of other seals and the closely related sea lions. In 1870 the U.S. government granted an exclusive concession to the San Francisco–based Alaska Commercial Company to take seals on the Pribilofs. The company held the concession for two decades, effectively denying competitors access to the resource. As a result, two distinct sealing efforts developed: the shore-based hunt at the rookeries, primarily on the Pribilofs, and *pelagic* sealing, in which hunters aboard boats took animals at sea. The shore-based fishery is safer, more efficient, and results in far fewer wounded and dead animals lost.

While fur seals, like sea lions, have rotating hind flippers that enable them to walk on land, they move slower than people and can be herded easily. The hunters targeted the young, bachelor (non-breeding)

they returned to historic high levels by the 1990s. Meanwhile the Russians continued to harvest walruses in low numbers in the mid- to late 1900s, feeding most of the meat to captive foxes on farms. The Russian commercial hunt ended in 1992.

Native people on both sides of the Bering Sea still take walrus for subsistence—the meat is a highly valued food in some villages. Annual subsistence landings total fewer than 4,000 animals, but walruses struck and lost probably bring the total removals to 6,000-7,000. These numbers

A cat and an arctic fox exchange looks at St. Paul.

As early as the 1870s, biologists observed the decrease in native birds due to predation by introduced foxes.

males, which were herded onto beaches or grassy areas, selected, and dispatched with a club to the head.

The brutally efficient seal hunts decimated the stocks, which had stood as high as three million when the commercial hunt began. The International Fur Seal Treaty of 1911 ended pelagic sealing.

Even after the commercial seal hunts ended, the U.S. government maintained a smaller sealing operation in the Pribilofs, to provide employment for Aleut hunters and revenue to help support the isolated Pribilof communities. Until the carnage finally ended in the 1950s, tens of thousands of young male seals were taken from the herds each year.

A small subsistence hunt continues to this day, providing meat, bait, and pelts which local people make into merchantable clothing and handicrafts. The local tribal body works with university and federal agencies to maintain research and manage these stocks.

Top—An arctic fox pup and mother nuzzle each other on St. Paul Island. Bottom—A fox farm sits deserted at Lorino, Russia.

Fox farms

As the profitability of sea otters diminished, first Russian and then Native hunters turned to other furbearers. They began to hunt native foxes, land otters, beavers, wolves, and other animals of the region.

The next logical step was fur farming. In the last years of the nineteenth century a number of fox farms were established on both sides of the sea. "Farm" really overstates the situation; in many cases blue foxes were simply released on remote islands and left to fend for themselves.

And fend they did, often eradicating local seabird populations. As early as the 1870s, biologists observed the decrease in native birds due to predation by introduced foxes. In some cases mice or ground squirrels also were introduced to Aleutian islands to provide food for foxes, and those rodents had their own impacts on the native biota.

A century later the U.S. Fish and Wildlife Service, manager of most of the lands in the Aleutians, still conducts a fox extermination program to rid the islands of imported bird predators. Some species of birds, most notably the Aleutian Canada goose, have responded well to the efforts, rebuilding their population from the brink of extinction.

Sheep and cattle also were introduced to the Aleutians, and the Fish and Wildlife Service later had to conduct feral cattle eradication. Today, rats are a growing concern. They can reach isolated islands via ships.

THE FRESH HALIBUT FISHERY.

Halibut schooner under jib, foresail, and double-reefed mainsail. Nests of dories lashed on deck amidships. Rigged for fall and winter fishing. (Sect. v, vol. i, p. 7.)

Drawing by Capt. J. W. Collins.

Commercial fisheries

As valuable as the sea mammal industries were, they have been dwarfed by commercial fisheries. Tens of thousands of people work catching and processing fish and shellfish, and tending to the vessels and processing plants. The annual value of the fisheries is over a billion dollars on the American side alone.

Dory schooner fishery

The cod fishery started in the 1870s. Picturesque three- and four-masted schooners sailed north from San Francisco, Seattle, and Vancouver, their decks stacked with nested dories (small flat-bottom rowboats). A single man oper-

ated each dory, rowing, sailing, and cranking a hand-powered gurdy (winch) to retrieve short setlines deployed for cod, and later for halibut. It was brutal, dangerous work, but profitable because of a strong market in Europe for split and salted cod.

Foreign fleets

The first cod fishing shore stations were built in 1909 and the dory schooner fishery ended in the 1930s. Starting in the late 1940s first Japanese and then Russian, Polish, and Korean distant water trawlers began working the Bering Sea. These fleets were highly effective at catching fish, and numerous stocks were depleted during that era. Landings data are hard to come by, but all indications are that huge quantities were taken during a more than 30-year

Walleye pollock.

Billions of pounds of pollock are harvested from the Bering Sea each year.

period. Cod was one of many species targeted by the build-up of foreign vessels that fished those waters after World War II.

The foreign fleets had a lot of other resources in their sights as well. Pollock, sablefish, halibut, yellowfin sole, atka mackerel, herring, Pacific ocean perch, and king crab were taken by trawl gear, on longlines, in gillnets and tangle nets, and in pots. Some distant water fleets in those days conducted *pulse fishing*—the fleet hammered a particular stock in a particular region to the point that it was no longer economically viable to fish it, and then moved on to another location or shifted to another species. There was no pretense of conservation.

A large Japanese high seas drift gillnet fleet in the southern Bering Sea and northern Gulf of Alaska intercepted Alaska-bred salmon by the hundreds of millions during those years, contributing to a depletion of stocks. That depletion, combined with climate change, which also contributed to the crash of salmon stocks, left few salmon for inshore American fishermen in some districts.

Initially the fishery was specifically for salmon but in later years the Japanese companies claimed to be targeting squid with their drift nets, and landing salmon only as bycatch. American and Canadian negotiators, working through treaty processes, gradually pushed the drift net fleets westward far enough that the impact on Alaska salmon was reduced, if not eliminated, and Alaska salmon stocks rebounded. Finally, in the 1990s, all high seas drift net fishing in the North Pacific was banned, but the other fleets fished on without restraint.

Fishery Conservation and Management Act

The most profound change in the world's commercial ocean fisheries occurred with the establishment of 200-mile exclusive zones, originally called fishery conservation zones (FCZs) and later exclusive economic zones (EEZs). The U.S. FCZ was part of the federal Fishery Conservation and Management Act (FCMA) of 1976, now commonly known as the Magnuson-Stevens Act. The United States wasn't the first country to establish one; Canada preceded the United States by a year and some

A midwater trawler hauls in a catch of pollock on the Bering Sea.

NATALIE FOBES ©

South American countries had declared 200-mile exclusive zones more than a decade earlier. But the U.S. zone probably had the biggest impact in the number of foreign fleets displaced, and many other countries subsequently established similar zones, including the Soviet Union.

The FCMA did several things, including establishing the eight regional fishery management councils, but the most dramatic result was the start of the "Americanization" process in the FCZ. Foreign vessels were allowed to take only that part of the TAC (total allowable catch) of a given stock that was left after American boats had taken what they could, and foreign processors could take delivery only of catch that American processors couldn't use. The immediate result was a rapid buildup of American catcher boats, displacing foreign catchers and delivering to foreign processors under so-called "joint venture" arrangements. American

fishermen quickly demonstrated that they could catch the entire TACs of most species, and soon after American processors (often with foreign financing) showed that they could utilize the catch. In less than a decade after Congress passed the FCMA the foreign fleets were out of the American 200-mile zone in the Bering Sea, as well as in the Pacific, Atlantic, and Gulf of Mexico.

Bottomfish fleet

The fishing power of the modern bottomfish fleet is awesome. Individual vessels range from 60 to as much as 300 feet in length (20-100 m), with engines developing from about 400 to 4,000 horsepower. Bottom trawlers, or *draggers*, tow nets as much as 200 feet wide and up to 12 feet high (70 × 4 m) along the bottom. Heavy steel plates called "doors" are set at the outer ends of the mouth of the net and angled so that the water pressure on their surfaces from the motion through the sea

MANDY MERKLEIN ©

A Polish joint venture trawler in the Bering Sea.

Larger trawlers can catch as much as 100 tons of fish in a single tow, and factory trawlers catch and process in a continuous operation without returning to shore for weeks at a time.

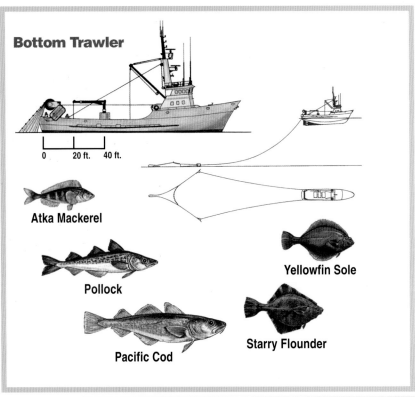

Bottom Trawler

0   20 ft.   40 ft.

Atka Mackerel

Pollock

Pacific Cod

Yellowfin Sole

Starry Flounder

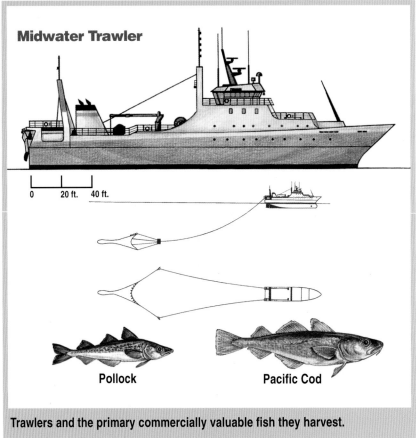

Midwater Trawler

0   20 ft.   40 ft.

Pollock

Pacific Cod

Trawlers and the primary commercially valuable fish they harvest.

Culture and Commerce

Sockeye salmon mill about in their final spawning phase in Iliamna Lake after migrating upriver from the Bering Sea.

forces them outward to spread the net.

The trawl doors plow grooves in the substrate as the heavy chain or rubber disk footrope scrapes the surface, and the net pretty much captures everything in its path. *Midwater* trawlers use even bigger nets— as much as 240 feet wide and 180 feet high (80 × 60 m), but their doors don't normally contact the bottom. Instead the boat operators "fly" their nets up in the water column, adjusting their speed to raise or lower the nets to intercept schools of fish located by the vessel's sophisticated electronics. Larger trawlers can catch as much as 100 tons of fish in a single tow, and factory trawlers catch and process in a continuous operation without

returning to shore for weeks at a time.

Salmon fishery

The inshore fisheries evolved separately from offshore fisheries. The salmon canning industry started in California and worked its way north to the Columbia River, Southeast Alaska, and eventually to the muddy shores of Bristol Bay in the 1890s. Canning developed as an efficient way of preserving food so that it could be cheaply transported long distances, kept indefinitely, and used to support armies in the field.

The first canneries on the Bering shore were on Nushagak Bay, but soon all the river systems in Bristol Bay had

canneries. Supplying fish to them sustained a fleet that numbered around two thousand small boats and hundreds of shore-based setnetters. Those fisheries continue to operate today, though in somewhat different configurations. A few of the canneries still operate too, but about half the salmon caught in Bristol Bay now is frozen, in shore plants or aboard huge floating factory freezer ships, and some is flown out fresh to markets in the United States and Japan.

Until the 1950s a few mostly Seattle-based companies owned not only the canneries but also the boats and gear, and hired the fishermen as employees who could be ordered about or fired. Fishing in Bristol Bay

Sockeye salmon from Bristol Bay.

The biggest herring in North America spawn in certain bays on the Bering Sea coast, and the largest single stock spawns in several bays near Togiak.

was done, as required by law, with gillnets from small wooden sailboats that were towed to and from the grounds by diesel-powered "monkey boats." When the sailboat-only law was changed in 1951 fishermen put small gasoline engines in their sailboats, which made them safer and more versatile. Soon fishermen were buying their own boats, which were designed for power and which gave them the ability to move from district to district and company to company.

The heyday of the independent fisherman had arrived, and fishermen have never looked back. Now Bristol Bay boats may cost upwards of a quarter million dollars, sport thousand-horsepower engines, and are capable of travel at 30 knots. For more than a decade high fish prices and abundant runs supported this kind of investment,

but world markets are changing and the value of the fishery is down. Expectations in Bristol Bay are more modest now.

Farther up the coast, the Alaska-Yukon-Kuskokwim salmon fishery wasn't much more than a commercialization of traditional subsistence skiff fisheries until the late 1970s, when escalating fish prices supported new interest and new investments. The boom was short-lived, however. Now participation in AYK salmon fisheries is small, and few if any fishermen make a living off them.

Herring fishery

Likewise, changes in Japanese import law resulted in a herring boom in the 1970s, 1980s, and 1990s. Japanese importers want the fish for their roe—it is brined for a holiday delicacy called *kazunoko*. The biggest herring

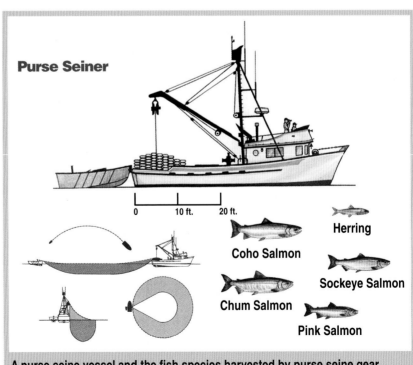

A purse seine vessel and the fish species harvested by purse seine gear.

Culture and Commerce

in North America spawn in certain bays on the Bering Sea coast, and the largest single stock spawns in several bays near Togiak. Fishermen use either purse seines to wrap up schools of herring, or anchored gillnets which snag the fish as they approach the rocky shoreline to spawn. For a few years hundreds of western Alaska villagers were able to profit from the herring fishery, but it, too, has fallen victim to depressed market conditions.

Crab fishery

The crab fishery has had its boom and now its bust. The problem with crab is not market conditions, but environmental conditions that affect the productivity of the stocks. Fishermen deploy crab pots, big cages ($7 \times 7 \times 4$ feet; $2.3 \times 2.3 \times 1.3$ m) containing bait jars, to catch the crab. In the peak years almost every pot came up crammed with crab and still more were hanging on the outside. In the late 1970s American vessels landed as much as 180 million pounds of king crab (90,000 tons), and a few years later up to 300 million pounds of opilio Tanner (snow) crab (150,000 tons). Both stocks subsequently plummeted and landings in recent years have been ten percent of their record highs.

No one quite understands the cause of the crab crash. Taking only males of a size such that they could have spawned at least once should have made the harvest sustainable. But many female and undersized males were killed by handling on deck, parasites

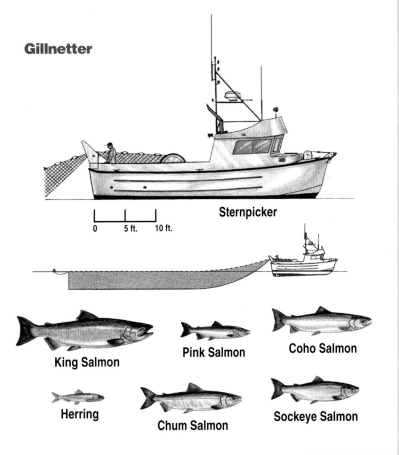

Top—Gillnetters on Bristol Bay swarm over a group of migrating sockeye salmon. Bottom—A gillnet vessel and the fish species this gear type harvests.

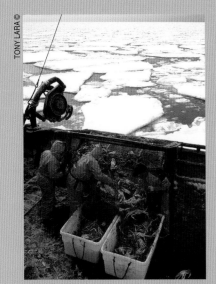
Bering Sea snow crab
and pan ice.

At the same time
that Alaska's crab
and shrimp crashed,
two of their major
predators—cod and
pollock—flourished,
and there may be
a connection.

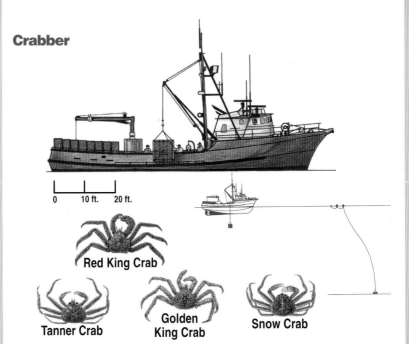

Crabber

0   10 ft.   20 ft.

Red King Crab

Tanner Crab

Golden
King Crab

Snow Crab

Top—Crab fishermen haul in a pot containing snow crab from the Bering
Sea. The crab will be kept alive in holds until the vessel returns to port.
Bottom—A typical Bering Sea crabber and the crab this gear type harvests.

Culture and Commerce

and disease probably were a factor, and changes in ocean temperature likely played a role. At the same time that Alaska's crab and shrimp crashed, two predators—cod and pollock—flourished. Scientists think there may be a connection.

Changing fisheries

The Bering Sea's fisheries are by no means dead, but they are changing, and in some respects the glory days are gone. But the Bering Sea still supports America's biggest and most valuable commercial fishery, Alaska pollock, as well as numerous other fisheries that employ thousands of people both inside and outside the region.

Creation in the mid-1990s of the Community Development Quota (CDQ) system resulted in some of the wealth of those fisheries being shared with cash-poor communities along the Bering Sea coast, countering some of the impact of other declining fisheries.

A short-lived gold rush

The waning years of the nineteenth century saw prospectors and adventurers dispersed across much of the far north of the North American continent searching for sources of wealth, be it minerals, furs, or anything else of value. A few found it in the form of gold, and several gold rushes occurred almost simultaneously at different locations.

Most famous was the

The Nome beach bustles with action during the gold rush around 1899. The Snake River is visible at the upper left background. Tents dotted the beach for 30 miles at the peak of the gold rush.

Klondike rush of 1898, which took thousands of gold seekers into the Yukon Territory. Many of them reached the gold fields by Yukon River steamers, departing from St. Michael on Norton Sound.

Others found their pot of gold at nearby Cape Nome, just across Norton Sound from St. Michael. Also in 1898 three Scandinavian prospectors discovered gold in the beach sands and triggered a smaller gold rush. The tiny village of Nome blossomed into a tent city of 20,000, and the shoreline and nearby river valleys soon were dotted with huge gold dredges. The boom was short lived, but gold seekers still return to Nome to try their luck on the beaches or, more

commonly now, in the shallow waters off Nome's shores. There they use floating suction dredges to bring bottom sediments to the surface to be sifted for tiny flakes of gold. It's certainly no bonanza, and few if any are even making a living at it, but Nome's remaining gold dredgers are a dedicated cadre of hardy individuals who apparently get enough out of it to make it worthwhile.

Other locations contain mineral deposits as well, like the platinum deposits adjacent to Goodnews Bay, and the cinnabar (mercury ore) mines that once operated up the Wood River off Bristol Bay. But the hope of great mineral wealth largely has faded from the shores of the Bering Sea.

U.S. military cemetery in the Aleutians.

Not all Americans realize it, but the only place, since the War of 1812, that American territory has been attacked and occupied by a foreign power is a remote part of the western Aleutians.

World War II and Cold War years

During World War II and the Cold War era, military installations and operations altered parts of the Bering Sea coastal landscape on both sides, with troop and air bases, early warning radar installations, and naval facilities. The Aleutians even became part of the Pacific Theater of Operations during the dark early days of World War II.

World War II

Not all Americans realize it, but the only place, since the War of 1812, that American territory has been attacked and occupied by a foreign power is a remote part of the western Aleutians. In June of 1942 Japanese naval aircraft staged raids on the small U.S. Navy base at Dutch Harbor, killing dozens of servicemen and destroying much of the facility. A few days later Japanese troops landed on Kiska and Attu islands and began an occupation that required months of fierce fighting by U.S. Army troops to dislodge.

The Aleutian Campaign was dubbed the "Thousand Mile War," because the Aleutian island chain stretches across the Pacific Ocean about 1,000 miles. Historians have characterized the Japanese assault on the Aleutians either as a diversionary tactic to distract American forces from Japan's real objectives in the southern Pacific, or as an attempt to launch a stepping-stone advance up the Aleutian chain to the American mainland.

P-38 Lightnings sit ready for combat on an under-construction airfield in the Aleutian Islands during World War II. While U.S. Army Air Corps pilots engaged in lethal combat with the Japanese forces, bad flying conditions were the cause of more aviator casualties than was combat.

1. U.S. soldiers watch their comrades push up a hill on Attu Island as their landing craft closes on the beach.
2. Navy nurses are greeted by Air Corps officers at Kiska Island. 3. Dutch Harbor burns after a Japanese air raid in 1942.
4. U.S. soldiers await action on an Aleutian island. 5. A P-40 Warhawk fighter taxis on a dirt airstrip in the Aleutians.

In either case, the thousands of casualties on both the American and Japanese sides were real, and hardware and materiel from that conflict still litter the landscape and continue to contaminate the environment.

A little known element of that conflict was the internment of hundreds of Aleut people in camps in Southeast Alaska, ostensibly for their own protection. Many of the internees, housed in crude, poorly heated barracks for years, died of diseases brought on by the damp rainforest climate. Those who survived returned to their villages to find their homes looted or destroyed. Many people displaced by the war never returned to permanent lives in the Aleutians but instead relocated to other parts of Alaska or the United States. The Aleuts interned in Alaska fared no worse than the Attuans captured by the Japanese. Some who were sent to work camps on the Japanese mainland weren't able to return until after the war ended in 1945.

During World War II the United States and Soviet Union were allies. The Bering Strait was part of the route that the two governments used to transport *Lend-Lease* military aircraft from American factories to Soviet aviators, who flew them into combat against Axis forces. Fairbanks was a major staging area, and small airstrips were located throughout the Alaska Interior and out to Nome. On the Russian side, corresponding airstrips are still visible at strategic locations.

"Tin City," a U.S. radar installation on Little Diomede Island.

Amchitka Island in the Aleutians was the site of three underground nuclear tests, in 1965, 1969, and 1971, which included the largest hydrogen bomb blast ever detonated.

The Cold War

After World War II, the United States and Soviet Union, capitalist and socialist nations fearful of one another, engaged in the 50-year-long Cold War. The "Ice Curtain" separated the lands on two sides of the Bering Sea. The term is a paraphrase of Winston Churchill's famous expression "Iron Curtain" which referred to the political and military frontier separating Eastern and Western Europe.

In the Bering Sea, Native communities that previously had been free to trade across the Bering Strait were cut off from one another, and families were split up. Warships of both nations patrolled Bering Sea waters to reinforce national sovereignty. U.S. air bases at places like King Salmon and Galena launched fighter interceptors to ensure that no Soviet aircraft strayed into American air space. A major naval base was built on Adak Island, which remained operational until 1995. The U.S. coastline was dotted with "White Alice" DEW Line (Distant Early Warning) radar sites designed to detect Soviet aircraft or intercontinental ballistic missiles headed toward America.

A tragic event occurred in 1983 which reinforced the high degree of fear represented by the Ice Curtain. A Korean civilian airliner, en route from Anchorage to Seoul, apparently strayed off course and into Soviet airspace off Kamchatka. The airliner left Soviet airspace over the Okhotsk Sea but re-entered off Sakhalin Island, where Soviet interceptor jets shot it down, killing 269 people.

A large component of the Soviet Union's submarine fleet, containing both conventional and nuclear vessels, was based at Petropavlovsk-Kamchatsky and at a super-secret base farther up the Kamchatka coast. The airport at Yelizovo, outside Petropavlovsk, was a major air force installation, and a deactivated fleet of combat aircraft for many years could be seen on the tarmac there.

Cold War science

Alaska had a significant role in the nuclear age. A site near Cape Thompson was proposed for creation of a harbor by use of a nuclear explosion. The blast never was authorized, but the Atomic Energy Commission did research in the area on the health effects of low levels of exposure to nuclear radiation. Amchitka Island in the Aleutians was the site of three underground nuclear tests, in 1965, 1969, and 1971, which included the largest hydrogen bomb blast ever detonated. Scientists are still measuring environmental radioactivity in the area. Concern over Amchitka testing was a factor in establishment of the environmental group Greenpeace.

Only scientists, it seems, were able to breach the ideological wall that separated the two sides, and even they were successful only on a limited basis. As far back as the 1930s, archeologists and anthropologists had crossed over to work with their colleagues, and information

USAF ©

An Alaska-based U.S. Air Force F-15 Eagle shadows a Soviet Tu-95 Bear long-range bomber and missile platform off the Alaska coast. Many intercepts were conducted during the Cold War years.

was shared freely. After World War II oceanographic and fisheries science flourished and tentative early steps were taken by scientists to work together. As early as the late 1940s and early 1950s biologists and oceanographers were conducting joint projects and working together at labs and aboard ships.

Cold War ends

The reforms known as *glaznost* ("openness") and *perestroika* ("restructuring"), which characterized the policies of Commu-

nist Party General Secretary (and later Soviet Union President) Mikhail Gorbachev from 1985 to 1991, started the process of opening the channels of Bering Sea trade and communication. By 1990 charter flights operated between Nome and Providenya, and in 1991 there were flights between Anchorage and other Soviet Far East cities.

With the dissolution of the Soviet Union at the end of 1991 the floodgates were flung open so that trade and travel of many kinds blossomed. Several regular flights per week were

scheduled between Anchorage and Russian Far East cities. People from the oil and timber industries, fishermen, entrepreneurs, and missionaries flooded into Russia. Many headed for Bering Sea ports and administrative and supply centers for the Bering Sea. Tourists flocked in on budget-priced air tours, or flew to exclusive hunting and fishing lodges aboard repainted MI-8 Soviet helicopters. Russian students and trainees, some of them from remote coastal towns, came to Alaskan and other American colleges to learn business and technology.

Cooperation

Now U.S. Coast Guard and Russian Border Guard officers tour each other's ships and coordinate fisheries enforcement in the Bering Sea. The White Alice radar sites are closed (replaced by more sophisticated satellite monitoring), the Air Force has pulled out of King Salmon, and the Bear bombers and nuclear subs are mothballed at Petropavlovsk.

Russian and American presidents have declared the two nations friends. With luck, another ice age in Russian-American relations is not on the horizon. But the Bering Sea's strategic location at the juncture of two huge continents and mighty nations is sure to keep it under constant military surveillance. And if the global climate continues to warm and the arctic ice pack continues to retreat, the Bering Sea's potential as a shipping route will further increase its strategic importance.

Watching walruses on Round Island.

Many "cultural" tourists fly to Nome to see relics of the gold rush, or descend on any of the dozens of Native villages that welcome visitors.

A fisherman casts under the midnight sun on the Kisaralik River near Bethel.

Tourism

If any event signaled the start of the Bering Sea tourism industry, it probably was the 1899 Harriman Expedition. Organized by a U.S. East Coast industrialist, the cruise aboard a chartered ship took scientists, writers, artists, and politicians up the Gulf of Alaska coast and into the Bering Sea, reaching as far north as St. Lawrence Island. The party observed wildlife, visited villagers who had rarely seen Westerners, and looted cultural sites for souvenirs. A century later many of the artifacts taken by expedition members were returned to their rightful owners. Although through ignorance they committed some classic errors, they were in essence the precursors of today's cultural and ecotourists.

Culture and Commerce

A rainbow trout caught in the Kisaralik River.

Recreational hunting and fishing

It was half a century, however, before tourism really started catching on, and when it did the visitors were mainly fishermen and hunters. In the post-war years Southwest Alaska became known as a sportsmen's mecca. Angling for rainbow trout, Dolly Varden, and salmon in Katmai and the entire Bristol Bay region became legendary. Trophy caribou, moose, and bears drew nimrods from around the world. Soon the Arctic-Yukon-Kuskokwim area and locations north of the Bering Strait drew anglers for pike, Arctic char, and sheefish, while hunters arrived to pursue walruses, muskoxen, and polar bears.

Sport hunting of walruses and polar bears, which are now under federal management, is no longer permitted. But the rod and gun set remains the most visible and lucrative component of western Alaska tourism.

Outdoorsmen arrived on Russia's eastern shores more recently, and in smaller numbers, although their relative economic influence may be just as great. Trout, steelhead, and salmon fishing are the biggest draw, and Kamchatka is the most popular destination, but hunters come in pursuit of the abundant brown bears and mountain sheep. The Far East also attracts anglers who want to fish for the giant salmon-like *taimen* (*Hucho hucho*), a fish that doesn't occur in Bering Sea watersheds. Kamchatka also lures mountaineers to the many volcanic peaks on the peninsula.

Visits to villages

Hook-and-shoot is only one component of the tourism industry. Many "cultural" tourists fly to Nome to see relics of the gold rush, or descend on any of the dozens of Native villages that welcome visitors. Opinions about tourism in Western Alaska communities tend to be polarized. Many residents see tourists as a source of ready cash and promise of a more prosperous future. Some villages perform cultural dances, offer Native food dinners, and promote sale of locally made arts and crafts, especially carved walrus ivory, grass baskets, and sewn skin items.

Other residents consider visitors to be intruders who violate their privacy, impart unwholesome values on their youth, and compete for fish and game or at least for prime fishing and hunting locations. Some villagers object to catch-and-release fishing, which they consider offensive to the spirits of the fish that willingly give themselves for the sustenance of the people, and their views toward trophy hunting are even less charitable.

Ecotourism

The fastest-growing component of the industry is ecotourism, which focuses on wildlife and natural places, and espouses low-impact visitation. Ecotourism overlaps with rod-and-gun whenever a river rafter unlimbers a fly rod, and with cultural tourism when a visit is made to a Native village or fish camp. Ecotourism occurs at many levels, from the self-guided backpacker or kayaker to the passenger on a luxury "expedition" cruise ship.

Wildlife is the big draw for most ecotourists—brown bears at Katmai, walruses in Bristol Bay, and seabirds and

Hikers on
St. Matthew Island.

Young women perform a traditional dance for visitors in Lorino, Russia.

Storms are a problem all year, especially in fall and winter, and ice halts water-borne traffic for almost half the year along most of the U.S. coastline of the Bering Sea.

fur seals in the Pribilofs. But other features attract as well, including the volcanic caldera of Aniakchak on the Alaska Peninsula and the broad and historic Yukon River itself. An emerging ecotourism focal point is the Bering Land Bridge National Preserve, which encompasses 2.7 million acres on the northern Seward Peninsula. This area is planned for inclusion in a future Beringian Heritage International Park, which will eventually include components on both sides of the Bering Sea. The Bering Land Bridge National Preserve includes tundra and Chukchi Sea coastline rich in migratory waterfowl and marine mammals, as well as historical and cultural sites.

The Beringian region, which is culturally and ecologically connected to the Bering Sea, encompasses a huge area,

from Russia's Kolyma River to Canada's McKenzie River in the Arctic to Kamchatka and the Alaska Peninsula in the south. Although the Russian and American presidents signed an agreement to create a Beringian international park in 1990, the congresses of the two nations did not follow through with enabling legislation. The focus of Beringian tourism in the near term likely will be the Seward Peninsula, but when an international park finally is authorized and funded, it should draw tourists to the entire mainland coasts on both sides of the Bering Sea.

Transportation

Transportation is still highly problematic on the Bering Sea. No road or railroad connects with any other part of Alaska. No ferry or scheduled ship service provides passenger or vehicular access, other than the Alaska Marine Highway (state ferry) from Homer on Cook Inlet that makes several stops a year at False Pass, Akutan, and Dutch Harbor. Few towns have dock facilities to accommodate ships or ferries. Shallow water precludes ocean-going ships. Storms are a problem all year, especially in fall and winter, and ice halts waterborne traffic for almost half the year along most of the U.S. coastline of the Bering Sea.

No recreational boating facilities exist anywhere on the coast, and refueling points may be hundreds of miles apart. Special shallow draft tugs with barges, and landing craft, supply essential goods to coastal and upriver villages, but they do not carry passengers and their operations are constrained by sea and river conditions. Skiffs and other small boats are used extensively for personal transportation, subsistence, and small-scale commercial fishing and fish hauling. Many people get around in private single-engine planes, equipped with floats or with oversized "tundra tires" that can land on gravel beaches and treeless hillsides.

Scheduled commercial air service is expensive, usually more than a dollar a mile round-trip, and radiates out of Anchorage. A traveler who wants to go between two towns only one hundred air miles apart may have to fly in to Anchorage, change planes, and then fly out to the destination, covering 600 miles (1,000 km) or more in the process. Local ("bush") air

1. A commercial flight from Bethel unloads at Hooper Bay. The pickup truck serves as a taxi into town, accommodating people, luggage, and cargo. 2. The Alaska Marine Highway state ferry system operates a route from Homer to several stops along the Alaska Peninsula, out to Dutch Harbor. This one is shown docked at Akutan. 3. St. Paul has an active visitor industry focused on bird and fur seal watching.

travel is even more expensive, the cost driven in part by the price of insurance required to cover hazardous air taxi and bush plane operations. Air charters can easily run $10 per mile each way.

The situation in Russia is even more difficult because

there are few civilian fixed-wing aircraft, and few people affluent enough to support commercial air services.

While interest in tourism is growing, the Bering Sea will never see mass tourism unless a solution is found to the high cost of transportation.

Managing the Resources
CHAPTER SEVEN

C onsider the Bering Sea, and the vast watersheds on both sides. They total over a million square miles (2.6 million sq km) of some of the most remote and inhospitable sea and land in the world. The coastal area is inhabited by a small number of people, most of whom are poor and lack advanced technology. The bureaucratic structures necessary to manage those lands and waters may seem minimal, but in fact the area is swathed in multiple overlapping layers of administrative and regulatory bureaucracy. A bewildering plethora of acronyms signify the government agencies that manage, the national laws and international treaties that limit and direct the management, the non-government organizations that attempt to influence management, and the scientific institutes that contribute data and describe ecological relationships to support management. The complexity of Bering Sea natural resource management is most apparent in the commercial fisheries.

PA3 RUSS TIPPETTS/USCG©

A boarding team from the U.S. Coast Guard cutter *Jarvis*, homeported at the sprawling USCG base in Kodiak, awaits pick-up after completing a routine inspection on a Bering Sea crabber.

Fisheries Management

FCMA

Until the 1976 passage of the Fishery Conservation and Management Act (FCMA) Bering Sea fisheries were relatively unregulated. The State of Alaska managed fisheries out to three miles (4.9 km) from shore, mainly the salmon harvests that took place in the rivers and bays, but had no jurisdiction beyond that point. The federal Territorial Sea—a legal extension of national sovereignty to a portion of the adjacent sea—was

Left—A Bering Sea midwater trawler hauls in a hefty catch of pollock.

NATALIE FOBES ©

An ADFG seasonal worker mends a gillnet used to monitor salmon abundance.

The practice of "fisheries management" is really people management with respect to their exploitation of fish.

established at six miles in 1958 and extended to 12 miles (19.5 km) in 1982. It prevented foreign fleets from fishing right up to the coastline. The International Pacific Halibut Commission regulated halibut landings. Few American vessels fished out in the Bering Sea. Under international law and maritime tradition, freedom of the seas meant that coastal states could not restrict the activities of vessels of other nations on the high seas.

The FCMA changed all that when the United States unilaterally declared domain over fisheries out to 200 nautical miles from shore (325 km), which encompasses almost half of the Bering Sea. Within a few years every coastal nation worldwide had done the same, including the Soviet Union which claimed most of the other half of the Bering Sea. Only the "Donut Hole," a few thousand square miles in the middle, outside both U.S. and Soviet jurisdiction, remained free of coastal state control.

Regional management councils

The Fishery Conservation and Management Act did more than simply declare sovereignty over the 200-mile zone. It also created a management structure to exercise that sovereignty. The structure is based around eight regional fishery management councils. The one that manages fisheries in the Bering Sea and Gulf of Alaska waters is the North Pacific Fishery Management Council (NPFMC), based in Anchorage. The council has 11 voting members appointed by the

U.S. President, supported by scientific and industry advisory committees plus professional staff.

The council entertains proposals, hears public testimony, debates the merits of various amendments, and writes fishery management plans for all the commercially exploited species under its jurisdiction. It sets limits on bycatch, establishes total allowable catch (TAC) quotas, and devises schemes for allocating catch among user groups. It also administers a quota share system for allocating halibut and sablefish catches, and administers the division of landings among different classes of processors. The council's decisions are crafted into recommendations and then forwarded to the U.S. Secretary of Commerce for approval. If approved, they go to NOAA Fisheries for implementation and enforcement.

NOAA Fisheries

NOAA Fisheries, until 2003 called the National Marine Fisheries Service (NMFS), is part of the National Oceanic and Atmospheric Administration, Department of Commerce. NOAA Fisheries employs biologists and statisticians to collect and analyze fishery data; lawyers, economists, and anthropologists to write regulations and analyze their effects; and enforcement officers to ensure that the regulations are followed. NOAA Fisheries uses test fishing, reports from fishery observers, and mathematical modeling to determine stocks of fish and to calculate catch quotas.

NOAA Fisheries enforce-

State and Federal Management of Alaska Fisheries

Management of Alaska commercial fisheries is complicated. Depending on location, some species are managed by either federal or state agencies, and some are managed internationally through treaties with other countries. Following is the general management responsibility by species.

State Managed

Chinook salmon	*Oncorhynchus tshawytscha*
Sockeye salmon	*Oncorhynchus nerka*
Coho salmon	*Oncorhynchus kisutch*
Pink salmon	*Oncorhynchus gorbuscha*
Chum salmon	*Oncorhynchus keta*
Pacific herring	*Clupea pallasii*
Pacific cod	*Gadus macrocephalus*
Rockfishes*	*Sebastes & Sebastolobus* sp.
Lingcod	*Ophiodon elongatus*
Snow crab	*Chionoecetes opilio*
Tanner crab	*Chionoecetes bairdi*
Grooved Tanner crab	*Chionoecetes tanneri*
Triangle Tanner crab	*Chionoecetes angulatus*
Golden king crab	*Lithodes aequispinus*
Red king crab	*Paralithodes camtschaticus*
Blue king crab	*Paralithodes platypus*
Scarlet king crab	*Lithodes couesi*
Dungeness crab	*Cancer magister*
Korean hair crab	*Erimacrus isenbeckii*
Weathervane scallop	*Patinopecten caurinus*
Snails	*Neptunea* sp.
Giant Pacific octopus	*Octopus dofleini*
Sea cucumber	*Parastichopus californicus*
Green sea urchin	*Strongylocentrotus droebachiensis*
Spot shrimp	*Pandalus platyceros*

State Managed (continued)

Northern (pink) shrimp	*Pandalus borealis*
Coonstriped shrimp	*Pandalus hypsinotus*
Sidestriped shrimp	*Pandalopsis dispar*
Littleneck clam	*Protothaca staminea*
Butter clam	*Saxidomus gigantea*
Pacific razor clam	*Siliqua patula*
Pacific geoduck	*Panopea abrupta*

Federally Managed

Arrowtooth flounder	*Atheresthes stomias*
Dover sole	*Microstomus pacificus*
Flathead sole	*Hippoglossoides elassodon*
Rock sole	*Pleuronectes bilineatus*
Yellowfin sole	*Pleuronectes asper*
Pacific halibut**	*Hippoglossus stenolepis*
Walleye pollock	*Theragra chalcogramma*
Sablefish (blackcod)	*Anoplopoma fimbria*
Skates	

* Frequently harvested in both state and federally managed fisheries.

** Managed jointly by the United States and Canada.

---

ment officers often patrol the seas in ships and aircraft of the U.S. Coast Guard, which is out there to enforce fishery, navigation, pollution, and safety laws.

NPFMC and NOAA Fisheries manage some aspects of the halibut fishery, to implement catch quotas imposed by the International Pacific Halibut Commission, and the quota share access limitation program.

ADFG

NPFMC and NOAA Fisheries cooperate on the management of some species—such as king and Tanner crab—with the State of Alaska. The Alaska Board of Fisheries makes regulations for salmon, herring, and other fisheries in state waters (inside three miles, 4.9 km). The Alaska Department of Fish and Game (ADFG) conducts research and fisheries monitoring. ADFG biologists can open and close fisheries in as little as two hours through provision for *emergency opening and closures.*

IFQs

The practice of "fisheries management" is really people management with respect to their exploitation of fish. Catch control is imposed on fishermen in several ways: limits on the times and locations for fishing, the type and amount of gear, the total amount of fish that can be caught (catch quotas), the total number of fishermen who may participate (license limitation), and the amount of catch allocated to each fisherman (quota shares or Individual Fishery Quotas— IFQs). Halibut and sablefish are managed under IFQs, and other species may eventually come under the same management system.

Halibut harvested in a CDQ fishery.

The CDQ program reserves some of the Bering Sea's bottomfish and crab total quotas for 32 Bering Sea coastal communities.

CDQ

The Community Development Quota (CDQ) program is a variant on IFQs. The CDQ program reserves some of the Bering Sea's bottomfish and crab total quotas for 32 Bering Sea coastal communities. The program provides access to the offshore fisheries for coastal residents, and to provide income via leasing or partnership arrangements with fishing companies. The communities, through their regional nonprofit fisheries development corporations, can invest in education and training for their residents and in village infrastructure.

The 32 villages have divided themselves into six regional fisheries economic development corporations and are banking income from joint venture arrangements with producers. Quota use arrangements usually require employment opportunities aboard catcher and processor ships and in corporate offices in addition to cash. The money has been invested in vessels, companies, and local infrastructure aimed at promoting the local fisheries through improved product handling and quality. The CDQ program is a major economic boon to the region.

Harvestable surplus

Unlike most fisheries, which are managed on the basis of quotas as a percentage of stock, salmon and herring are managed on the basis of *harvestable*

NOAA Fisheries runs a program whereby trained observers, paid by the fishing companies through contracting companies, are stationed aboard fishing vessels to monitor the catch. Above, two federal observers estimate the size of a pollock haul.

Managing the Resources

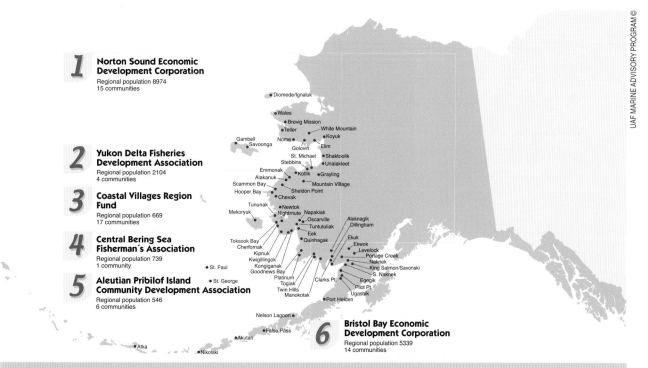

1 **Norton Sound Economic Development Corporation**
Regional population 8974
15 communities

2 **Yukon Delta Fisheries Development Association**
Regional population 2104
4 communities

3 **Coastal Villages Region Fund**
Regional population 669
17 communities

4 **Central Bering Sea Fisherman's Association**
Regional population 739
1 community

5 **Aleutian Pribilof Island Community Development Association**
Regional population 546
6 communities

6 **Bristol Bay Economic Development Corporation**
Regional population 5339
14 communities

The regional Community Development Quota system distributes some of the income from the rich offshore fisheries to tiny, cash-poor communities along the Bering Sea coast.

surplus. For every stock of fish there is a calculated optimum *escapement*, which is the number of spawners needed to sustain the stock at its *maximum sustainable yield* (MSY). Salmon fisheries are managed to allow the optimum escapement to pass through the fishing districts and into the spawning rivers, and then permit the fishermen to catch the rest. Escapement is determined by counters in streamside towers who tally spawners as they pass by, with in-river sonar counting devices, or by test fisheries conducted upstream from the commercial districts.

In the herring roe fishery, biologists have determined that between 10 and 20 percent of the total number of fish that arrive in the spawning districts can be taken each year without harming the stocks. Therefore, fishery managers set catch quotas based on the *observable biomass* they can see from spotter planes or on sonar.

Limited entry

Rather than using quota shares, which are not appropriate for salmon and herring fisheries, the state employs an access limitation or *limited entry* system for controlling the number of fishermen competing for resources.

Research

While NOAA Fisheries and ADFG are the main research organizations contributing to fishery management, there are others. Both the University of Alaska Fairbanks and University of Washington have major salmon research programs in the Bering Sea basin, and also conduct studies on other species. Land managers like the U.S. Fish and Wildlife Service and the National Park Service study freshwater and anadromous fish, particularly in parks and national wildlife refuges.

Fisheries management in Russia

Fisheries research and management are every bit as complicated on the Russian side of the Bering Sea. The primary research agency is the Pacific Ocean Institute of Research in

Russian fishermen empty a net of coho and chum salmon.

In recent years Russian and U.S. management and enforcement agencies have consulted with each other on management issues and have collaborated on enforcement.

Top—Representatives from the Russian Federal Border Service and the U.S. Coast Guard sign an agreement in Anchorage to bolster efforts to halt illegal fishing in the Bering Sea. Bottom—Petropavlovsk-Kamchatsky is home base for much of the research Russia conducts on Bering Sea fisheries.

Fisheries and Oceanography (the Russian language acronym is TINRO), with research centers in most of the Far Eastern regions. TINRO Centre in Vladivostok, and KamchatNIRO in Petropavlovsk-Kamchatsky, do most of the Bering Sea research. Scientists from the National Academy of Science and institutes in Moscow also participate.

Fishery management is a complex system of quotas authorized by the State Committee on Fisheries in Moscow and transferred to regional fisheries committees for allocation. Some quotas are sold at auction, while others are issued on the basis of qualifying history and performance. Primary enforcement is divided between Fisheries Inspection (*Rybvod*) and the national Border Guards, but Russian fishermen are subject to control and inspection by as many as eight agencies.

International cooperation

In recent years Russian and U.S. management and enforcement agencies have consulted with each other on management issues and have collaborated on enforcement. Of particular concern are vessels of third-party nations fishing in the unregulated Donut Hole, and overfishing stocks of both countries. Despite the improving U.S.-Russia cooperation, the American side continues to claim that Russians are overharvesting transboundary pollock (stocks that migrate back and forth across the international boundary), while the Russians claim that the international boundary enforced by the United States is incorrectly drawn and is depriving them of valuable pollock.

Merits of U.S. system

Fishermen often decry the "politics" of fisheries management, especially when decisions go against their interests. Applied science can indicate conservation requirements, but rarely can science solve an allocation problem. The relatively democratic process applied in the Bering Sea by the regional fishery management council and board of fisheries is in stark contrast to management systems elsewhere in the world.

It is not uncommon for civil servants or political appointees, thousands of miles removed from the fishing grounds and fishing communities, to make fisheries management decisions without direct user input.

Organizations

In the United States, agencies that manage resources are not omnipotent. Many associations and non-governmental organizations (NGOs) compete for influence over decisions. Where large sums of money are to be made the number and financial bases of these groups are largest.

Fisheries organizations

Fisheries associations are among the most influential in the Bering Sea. The Alaska Crab Coalition, Pollock Conservation Cooperative, Alaska Draggers Association, At-Sea Processors Association, Fishing Vessel Owners' Association, Groundfish Forum, Pacific Seafood Processors Association, United Catcher Boats, and United Fishermen's Marketing Association all represent segments of the catching and processing industries that try to influence fisheries management. Their attorneys and lobbyists attend North Pacific Fishery Management Council meetings, submit proposed regulation changes, testify on proposals of others, and work in other ways to bolster their members' position in the management process.

Inshore fishermen work

through the Alaska Independent Fishermen's Marketing Association, Bristol Bay Driftnetters Association, and other organizations to influence the Alaska Board of Fisheries process.

The Bering Sea Fishermen's Association protects the interests of Native commercial and subsistence users, as does the Yukon River Drainage Fisheries Association. The Bering Sea Coalition is a group of village leaders concerned with the Bering Sea environment.

Conservation groups

Marine conservation is big business, especially in the Bering Sea where the number of environmental groups with interests in management issues is growing. Some groups are focused on fisheries management, especially bycatch and the effects of trawling on habitat and species balance, while others are concerned about marine mammals and seabirds, coastal zone terrestrial habitat, climate change and global warming, and pollutants and contaminants.

The World Wildlife Fund and the Nature Conservancy of Alaska have had a Bering Sea conservation program for many years. Other groups that have Bering Sea programs include Center for Marine Conservation, Greenpeace, and the Audubon Society. World Wildlife Fund and Greenpeace also are active in Russia. The Alaska Marine Conservation Council promotes

A boarding party from the cutter *Jarvis* is lowered onto the Bering Sea.

The World Wildlife Fund and the Nature Conservancy of Alaska have had a Bering Sea conservation program for many years.

habitat protection, bycatch reduction, and the well-being of community-based small boat fleets. Conservation and allocation are often closely associated in fisheries management.

Native co-management

In recent decades resource management authority for some harvesting activities has been vested in organizations representing Alaska Native subsistence and commercial interests. The Kuskokwim salmon fishery is conducted under a co-management agreement with input from State of Alaska biologists and local fishermen. Goose hunting on the Yukon-Kuskokwim Delta is managed by a federal/Native co-management group under the Yukon-Kuskokwim Delta Goose Management Plan.

Under the Marine Mammal Protection Act only Alaska Natives have marine mammal hunting rights in Alaska, therefore co-management organizations with members from federal agencies and local communities control marine mammal hunting. The Eskimo Walrus Commission, the Alaska Beluga Whale Committee, the Alaska Eskimo Whaling Commission, and the Alaska Sea Otter and Harbor Seal Commission are co-management groups that oversee most of the eastern Bering Sea's subsistence marine mammal harvests.

Water and land management

Water management

Nobody owns the oceans beyond 12 miles (19.5 km) from shore, and under international law and maritime tradition, "innocent passage" of noncombatant vessels is unrestricted. The Coast Guard imposes safety, equipment, and manning requirements on foreign vessels entering U.S. waters, as well as on American vessels venturing out. The International Maritime Organization (IMO) exercises some management over shipping worldwide. The federal government, through agencies like NOAA Fisheries and U.S. Fish and Wildlife Service, controls the actions of mariners vis-à-vis marine wildlife, especially mammals and seabirds. The federal Minerals Management Service rules on applications to drill or mine the bottom in continental shelf waters. The International Whaling Commission regulates the subsistence whale hunt and prohibits commercial whaling. Numerous international treaties cover migratory waterfowl, polar bears, and other wildlife.

The state government has jurisdiction over submerged lands, which includes beaches up to the *mean high tide line* (the point reached by the average of all high tides). State authority extends to freshwater as well, including lake and river beaches and river bars that are submerged at least part of each year. However, for the purposes of management, the federal government assumes authority over "navigable" waters, although the definition of navigable varies with the issue. The list of waters deemed navigable for Coast-Guard licensing of vessel operators is much shorter than the list of navigable waters for federal subsistence management.

Land management

Ownership of Alaska coastal lands is a patchwork of federal, state, Native corporation, and private jurisdictions. With the exception of a few small military reservations, federal and state lands are held in trust for public uses, with some restrictions.

Federally owned lands

Most of the land on the Bering Sea coast is owned by the federal government and is in some form of protected status, including national wildlife refuges. The Alaska Maritime National Wildlife Refuge includes most of the Aleutians, the Pribilofs, and other islands and points on the mainland. The Togiak and Yukon Delta National Wildlife Refuges occupy a large chunk of Southwest Alaska from Dillingham on Bristol Bay to St. Michael on Norton Sound, and including Nunivak Island. Some federal land is managed by the Bureau of Land Management (BLM).

Native-owned lands

Within the borders of public land units are hundreds of smaller parcels or *inholdings* of private land. Most are owned by Native corporations or are *Native allotment*—authorized under the Alaska Native Claims Settlement Act and owned by individuals of Alaska Native ancestry. Originally the corporations were intended to preserve access to traditional family subsistence sites. But the corporation and individual allotments have gradually come to occupy most of the river and sea shoreline that is suitable

SEA SCIENCE

Partners in science

Understanding why populations thrive or decline is critical to people who depend on marine and terrestrial wildlife for food.

One way scientists can get clues to the health status of marine mammals and birds is to study tissues from dead (stranded) animals found on beaches or those taken by subsistence hunters. Tissue sampling is especially important when mysterious mass die-offs occur. But rarely are scientists around in remote parts of Alaska when carcasses are found or when animals are harvested, and so usually nothing is learned from the remains.

The North Pacific Marine Research (NPMR) program sponsored two related projects that tapped the skills of people in remote villages, to gather tissue samples from stranded marine mammals and birds. Local people were trained to record information about the stranded animal, such as cause of death (if obvious) and take tissue samples from dead animals. Depending on

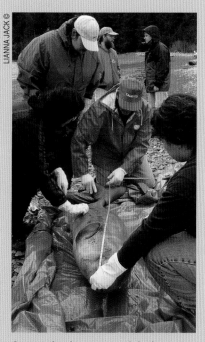

LIANNA JACK ©

A porpoise is measured during training in Seward, Alaska, aimed at engaging rural residents in marine mammal research.

the situation, they send the samples to laboratories for analysis or to the University of Alaska Museum for preservation and archiving.

This project also fosters good will between scientists and their Native partners, who for eons have accumulated knowledge about the local living resources.

A fishing lodge operating on wilderness rivers in a coastal wildlife refuge might have to deal with as many as 12 agencies to get permission to transit lands or establish "spike" (remote field) camps.

Solomon, Alaska, is a fish camp on the Solomon River 30 miles east of Nome and one mile north of Norton Sound. The seasonal camp is located on land owned by the Bering Strait Native Corporation.

for development or recreation. Some corporations manage lands to get revenue for shareholders. They lease campsites to sport fishing and hunting guides, and charge camping or day use fees for recreation. Some allotment holders lease pieces of their properties to lodges or fishing guide operations. Some allotments are mined for gravel, or subdivided into housing tracts.

Overlapping management

Other Bering Sea coastal lands are owned and managed by the State of Alaska, by local communities, and a very small amount by private individuals.

Sometimes management authorities overlap and conflict. For example, on federal lands the Fish and Wildlife Service, under direction of the regional subsistence board, manages subsistence fishing and hunting. Alaska Department of Fish and Game (ADFG), at the direction of the Board of Fisheries and Board of Game, manages sport fishing and hunting. Sometimes it takes a court case to determine whether a particular hunt is sport or subsistence.

A fishing lodge operating on wilderness rivers in a coastal wildlife refuge might have to deal with as many as 12 agencies to get permission to transit lands or establish "spike" (remote field) camps. The agen-

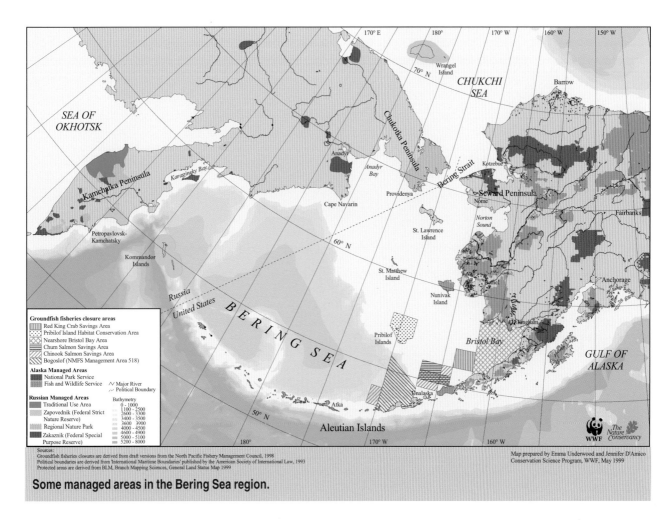

Groundfish fisheries closure areas
- ⫴ Red King Crab Savings Area
- ⬚ Pribilof Island Habitat Conservation Area
- ⬚ Nearshore Bristol Bay Area
- ⬚ Chum Salmon Savings Area
- ⬚ Chinook Salmon Savings Area
- ⬚ Bogoslof (NMFS Management Area 518)

Alaska Managed Areas
- ▪ National Park Service
- ▪ Fish and Wildlife Service
- ⋀ Major River
- ⋁ Political Boundary

Russian Managed Areas
- ▪ Traditional Use Area
- ▪ Zapovednik (Federal Strict Nature Reserve)
- ▪ Regional Nature Park
- ▪ Zakaznik (Federal Special Purpose Reserve)

Bathymetry
- 0 - 1000
- 1100 - 2500
- 2600 - 3300
- 3400 - 3500
- 3600 - 3900
- 4000 - 4500
- 4600 - 4900
- 5000 - 5100
- 5200 - 8000

Sources:
Groundfish fisheries closures are derived from draft versions from the North Pacific Fishery Management Council, 1998
Political boundaries are derived from International Maritime Boundaries' published by the American Society of International Law, 1993
Protected areas are derived from BLM, Branch Mapping Sciences, General Land Status Map 1999

Map prepared by Emma Underwood and Jennifer D'Amico
Conservation Science Program, WWF, May 1999

Some managed areas in the Bering Sea region.

cies might include the Coast Guard (boat operator and vessel licensing and equipment), the Federal Aviation Administration (aircraft operations), the U.S. Fish and Wildlife Service (refuge commercial use permits), fish and game boards over fishing and hunting regulations, ADFG, Alaska Department of Public Safety (Fish and Wildlife Protection), Alaska Department of Environmental Conservation (food service site inspection and waste disposal), Federal Communications Commission (radio station licenses), Alaska Department of Revenue (business licenses and taxes), Alaska Department of Labor (labor standards, workers compensation), Alaska Department of Natural Resources (use of river banks and bars and commercial use permits for state land), and Native corporations or individual allotment-holders.

Future of Bering coast land

Alaska is involved in a protracted conflict over the future of public lands and land management. On one side are those who believe too much land is "locked up" in public ownership, so that economic development is thwarted. Some politicians have made it their mission to divest the federal government, in particular, of as much of its lands as possible through programs to expand Native allotment, make "land swaps" to put more land in private ownership, and to lease lands to resource extractive industries. The other side views public lands as the national heritage to be preserved and protected from destructive exploitation. The good and bad of the Bering Sea coast is that very little of it has any potential economic value other than for recreation, so the debate has been less intense than elsewhere in the state, where timber, mineral, and oil and gas potential is greater.

Challenges
CHAPTER EIGHT

"The Bering Sea is Dying." So reads the banner headline of a regional tabloid newspaper. While that particular publication may be using hyperbole to boost its sales, it's not the only voice calling out that things are changing, and some changes might not be good for people and other species dependent on the cold northern ocean. Native hunters, commercial fishermen, ornithologists, biological oceanographers, political activists, and government bureaucrats all have sounded warnings about change in the Bering Sea.

The challenge is to determine the effects of changes, to what extent they are caused by human activity, and how to fix them or at least to help people and the ecosystem adapt.

Among the pressing issues in the Bering Sea that warrant attention in the near future are:

PAC ED MORETH/USCG ©

Workers clean oil from a beach at Dutch Harbor. The cargo ship *Swallow* ran aground there in 1989, spilling some of its fuel oil.

- The dramatic decrease in the numbers of Steller sea lions, nothern fur seals, sea otters, and other marine mammals, as well as seabirds.

- Changes in climate and weather, and their implications for biological productivity and for the suitability of the region for human habitation.

- Contaminants, including persistent organic pollutants, mercury and other heavy metals, and nuclear radiation.

- Conflicts among user groups over fisheries management.

- Drastically diminished value of some commercial fisheries, and the depressed coastal economies on both sides of the Bering Sea.

Left—Fog shrouding a seastack along the shore of Summit Island.
FRED HIRSCHMANN ©

169

The connection between pollock trawling and sea lion decreases is simplistic and appealing, but intensive research so far has not demonstrated direct cause.

A captive Steller sea lion cruises past a viewing window at the Alaska SeaLife Center in Seward. Scientists at the SeaLife Center conduct research to help solve the mystery of Western Alaska's sea lion declines.

Mammal and seabird declines

Steller sea lions

In 1997 the western stock of the Steller sea lion, including those in the Bering Sea, was declared endangered under the federal Endangered Species Act. In the 1960s about 300,000 of the big marine mammals roamed the North Pacific and Bering Sea, but by the late 1990s the count was down to around 60,000. Some stocks on the Russian side likewise have plummeted by as much as 90 percent. Projections are for the Western Alaska stock to become extinct sometime in the middle of the twenty-first century if the trend continues. At the same time, sea lions in Southeast Alaska and British Columbia slightly increased in numbers.

Causes natural or human?

Because of the perception that the valuable commercial fisheries affect sea lion populations, and because the Endangered Species Act mandates cessation of human activities that may drive endangered animals to extinction or prevent their recovery, a great deal of money and effort has been focused on determining the cause of the sea lion decline. Court decisions forced the National

Marine Fisheries Service (NOAA Fisheries) to prohibit fisheries around key sea lion rookeries, which cost some parts of the fishing industry dearly.

Scientists are investigating possible causes. They are looking at *bottom-up* (food resource) factors that affect health and condition of the animals, like non-lethal disease and pollution, fishery removals of important prey species, and a climate and/or regime shift that changed the forage fish composition of the sea. They are also looking at *top-down* (predator) factors that kill the animals, like subsistence hunting, shooting by fishermen, entanglement in fishing gear, predation by orcas and sharks, and lethal pollution or disease. A regime shift is a change in the relative importance of species in an ecosystem.

The role of pollock

In most of the western Gulf of Alaska and Bering Sea walleye pollock is the sea lion's number-one food item. Pollock also is the target of a huge and lucrative fishery, which annually takes more than a million metric tons of them from the American side of the Bering Sea alone. The connection between pollock trawling and sea lion decreases is simplistic and appealing, but intensive research so far has not demonstrated direct cause.

In fact, by some measures the trawlers may be the sea lion's best friend by harvesting the adult pollock—the primary consumers of juvenile pollock. This would leave more juvenile pollock for the juvenile sea lions to eat. Juvenile sea lions

are the ones that appear to be dropping out of the population.

On the other hand, it has been shown that although pollock are the largest component of sea lion diets, they are not the most nutritious. Some scientists believe that the abundance of pollock, displacing more nutritious herring, capelin, and sand lance, is causing the problem for sea lions. Some blame the shift in balance of forage fish species, caused by the near-extinction of great whales in Bering Sea waters.

The question is complicated by the fact that the rate of sea lion decline was greatest in the late 1980s and since then has slowed, so the causal factors may have changed. Whatever caused the decline may be different from the factors that prevent recovery. Recently

Left—A midwater trawler hauls in a net jammed full of walleye pollock from the Bering Sea. In different processed forms these fish are destined for domestic and foreign markets. Right—Deliveries of crab, pollock, and other groundfish make Dutch Harbor the nation's number-one port in volume of fish and shellfish landed each year.

Thick-billed murres and their eggs on Bogolsof Island.

Visitors to the Pribilof Islands draw the attention of fur seals.

In the latter half of the nineteenth century commercial hunting of northern fur seals reduced the population by 90 percent from a peak of about three million animals.

some research has shifted away from the food stress theory to look more closely at other top-down causes, including orca predation. Deprived of millions of tons of food by the intensive commercial whaling of the 1940s-1960s, orcas may have refocused their predatory habits to seals and sea lions. By one informed estimate, a shift of as little as 1% of orca predation could account for the disappearance of the sea lions. Big incidental kills of sea lions by trawl nets off Russia in the 1970s and 1980s could have severely damaged Alaska sea lion stocks.

Northern fur seals

Sea lions are not the only pinnipeds in trouble. Northern fur seals and harbor seals have experienced population declines nearly as precipitous. About 70 percent of the world's northern

fur seals breed on the Pribilof Islands, with smaller rookeries on the Kommandor Islands, Bogoslof Island, and at locations outside the Bering Sea.

In the latter half of the nineteenth century commercial hunting of northern fur seals reduced the population by 90 percent from a peak of about three million animals. After hunting was curtailed, about two million northern fur seals returned to the Pribilofs, followed by an inexplicable 50 percent drop in numbers. The Pribilof stock now is classified as depleted under the Marine Mammal Protection Act. Other stocks also are down, though not as dramatically as the Pribilof stock.

Harbor seals

Harbor seals occupy the Bering Sea coast only as far north as the normal winter ice edge, which in Alaska makes northern

Bristol Bay the limit of their range. At some haul-outs counts have declined little. At other locations, such as Nanvak Bay, the stock has dropped by 80 percent since the mid-1970s. Some haul-outs in the northern Pacific Ocean had similar declines. For both northern fur seals and harbor seals, scientists suspect that a change in availability of prey species is the likely cause for the declines.

Sea otters

While incidental catches by trawlers could explain the crash of sea lions and fur seals, they cannot account for the disappearance of sea otters, harbor seals, and numerous species of seabirds. The situation with sea otters in the Aleutians is particularly perplexing. Sea otters returned from near extinction to substantially repopulate their former range, and until the 1990s were at healthy sustained levels of nearly 100,000 animals. Then, inexplicably, they began to disappear from the western Aleutians, and by the end of the decade total count was down to 6,000. Since it is clear that people are not killing off the otters, scientists are looking at environmental explanations. The otters are known to have high levels of some pollutants, such as DDT, but the inquiry now is focused on a surprising suspect—killer whales. Some researchers believe that mammal-eating killer whales, deprived of seals and sea lion prey, have turned to eating the much smaller, nearly fat-free sea otters.

Top—A scientist catches a kittiwake in a study that examined how stress hormones in juvenile birds might affect their ability to survive as adults. Bottom—Murres also were studied to help determine why some Bering Sea avian populations thrive and others do not.

Seabirds

Some seabirds, including two species of murres and two species of kittiwakes, have seen marked declines in the last two decades, particularly at nesting areas such as the Pribilofs and eastern Aleutians. Seabird populations in Alaska are characterized by big fluctuations, and there is no way of knowing if numbers were stable before the current downturn. Cause of the current decrease is unclear but believed to be related to availability of prey.

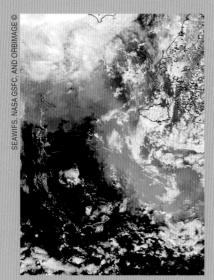

Plankton bloom along Alaska's Bering Sea coast.

Significant changes in the Bering Sea over the last 50 years are attributed to human activities.

Climate change

Theories abound for causes of steep declines in stocks of indicator species like sea lions and seabirds, as well as their inability to rebound. Much scientific inquiry has focused on atmospheric and seawater temperature, weather patterns and climate, and the effects of human-induced changes to the predator-prey balance.

Global warming

The effects of atmospheric warming, some subtle and some dramatic, are apparent worldwide, but nowhere more clear than in the sub-Arctic and Arctic. The boreal forest tree line is advancing northward, permafrost is melting, open water is appearing where only solid pack ice occurred previously, breakup is coming earlier, and the ice-free period is lasting later than at any time since data on such things have been kept by scientists. However, it is not clear if these effects are long-term and the result of *anthropogenic* (human caused) processes, or are related to natural climate cycles.

Under the prevailing view, *global warming* is a long-term, anthropogenic phenomenon that can only be reversed by significant changes in technology and behavior. This would result in smaller amounts of carbon dioxide and other "greenhouse gases" being released into the atmosphere. Although the subject of much debate, most scientists agree that 30 to 70 percent of the warming is due to fossil fuel combustion.

El Niño

El Niño is a short-term phenomenon that originates in the tropical western Pacific Ocean and causes higher temperatures in the sea and atmosphere for a year or two at a time. It affects local weather and can have dramatic temporary impacts on fish and wildlife. But El Niño is neither a cause nor result of global warming. Although El Niño is not a Bering Sea phenomenon, periods of extraordinarily warm weather there are associated with El Niño events in the North Pacific.

In an unprecedented 1997 bloom in the Bering Sea, and lesser events in 1998-1999, a dinoflagellate alga called *coccolithophore* proliferated and caused a massive seabird die-off. The bloom likely resulted from elevated seawater temperatures and a highly temperature-stratified water column. This condition first appeared during an El Niño year in the North Pacific, although it is not considered an El Niño–caused event.

Pacific decadal oscillation

Pacific decadal oscillation is a phenomenon characterized by increases and decreases of sea and air temperatures over a period of 19 or 20 years. Elevated sea temperatures, within limits, can be very beneficial to some species and harmful to others. The crab and shrimp crash of the late 1970s and 1980s that continues today accompanied an increase in sea temperatures; at the same time Alaska salmon, cod, and pollock flourished.

Regime shift

A *regime shift,* a change in the relative abundance of species, can have far-reaching consequences for an ecosystem. Climate change is strongly correlated with regime shifts. The regime shift that began around 1979, which coincided with increased water temperatures and decreased ice coverage, and continued to affect trophic relationships through the 1990s, is believed to be climate related. But climate isn't the only factor in regime shifts. Sometimes excessive fishing pressure or other factors can cause a shift in the ecological balance.

Cascade hypothesis

Significant changes in the Bering Sea over the last 50 years are attributed to human activities. One description of this process is called the *cascade hypothesis.*

Some scientists postulate that as a result of the near-extinction of several species of great whales, especially fin and sei whales during the 1950s and 1960s, huge volumes of plankton and small forage fishes were not eaten by the whales and therefore became available to support a pollock boom.

At the same time, a major groundfish fishery developed, targeting mid-trophic predators such as yellowfin sole and

A fin whale cruises the California coast. Some scientists think that the commercial harvest and resulting reduction in fin and sei whale populations may have led to a boom in the Bering Sea pollock population.

Pacific ocean perch which fed on plankton and small pelagic forage fish such as juvenile pollock.

Eventually the mid-trophic predators were overfished, leaving larger numbers of pollock. The combination of commercial activities released a great deal of food, reduced feeding competition, and diminished the number of predators, thereby allowing juvenile pollock to displace herring and sand lance as the dominant forage species. The thought is that this "top down" force allowed pollock to become the dominant species in the Bering Sea ecosystem.

Atmospheric forcing

Scientists are trying to find out whether *atmospheric forcing* through decadal oscillation, global warming, or other phenomena is imposing temperature and circulation changes that cause decreases in marine mammals and seabirds.

Further, they want to know if human-induced factors like whaling and selective fishing pressures played a bigger role. If environmental change in the Bering Sea is largely human-caused, theoretically it can be reversed over time. If it is caused by natural phenomena, there may be little people can do to bring back the species and restore the previous balance. A larger question managers are wrestling with is whether, and when, humans should intervene in changing an ecosystem.

Pollutants

Nobody is calling the Bering Sea "polluted" in the sense of discolored, malodorous, poisonous water. But certain contaminants have been identified in the fat and organs of fish and mammals that live in the Bering Sea. They fall into three general categories: *persistent organic pollutants* (POPs), heavy metals, and radioactive substances.

KURT BYERS/UAF ©

Rusting barrel at Hooper Bay.

Salmon from the Yukon River are known to have high levels of mercury in their flesh.

Persistent organic pollutants

POPs include a large number of toxic industrial products from DDT to dioxins and polychlorinated biphenyls. Some are used as pesticides, others as parts of manufacturing processes. POPs are slow to decompose in the environment, and *accumulate* in the fatty tissues of upper trophic level mammals, birds, and fish.

POPs are believed to originate in industrial centers and agricultural regions of the Pacific Rim continental land masses, and to be transported by wind, rivers, and ocean currents.

PCBs have been found in Bering Sea bottom sediments, and in plankton and *benthic fauna* (bottom dwelling animals). Some contaminants probably are accumulated from forage species that pick up the substances while feeding in the Pacific Ocean hundreds of miles south of the Aleutians. Detectable amounts of PCBs, DDT, and chlordanes, as well as the heavy metals butyl tin and mercury, have been measured in sea lion tissues.

Heavy metals

Mercury and cadmium are the two heavy metals found in the greatest abundance in Bering Sea animal tissues and in bottom sediments. Salmon from the Yukon River are known to have high levels of mercury in their flesh. Research now

SEA SCIENCE

Toxins in fish

As annual salmon returns decline in Western Alaska people there are shifting their attention more toward grayling, northern pike, and whitefish for food. As they do, scientists are taking a closer look at whether those fish contain toxic contaminants that might be unhealthy for people to consume. NPMR researchers tested pike and grayling from the Yukon River, and pike, grayling, and whitefish from the Kuskokwim River. They discovered tiny traces of mercury (a toxic heavy metal) in all species. Pike was the only one that had mercury levels higher than what the U.S. Food and Drug Administration considers as safe for eating.

STEPHEN JEWETT/UAF ©

A researcher pulls in a gillnet during a study on toxins in fish from Western Alaska rivers.

Waste disposal is a big challenge in isolated small, cash-strapped communities on both sides of the Bering Sea. 1 and 2. Fuel oil barrels rust away in Yanrakino, Russia. 3. A field serves as a general-purpose community dump site on St. Paul Island. 4. Inadequate waste handling practices by the U.S. military, and Soviet and U.S. nuclear tests, have contaminated sites in the Aleutians, Western Alaska, and the Bering Sea. Pictured here is a WWII military supply depot in the Aleutians.

indicates that some of the mercury in the Bering Sea food web actually comes from natural sources in the valleys of rivers that flow into the sea.

But that is not the whole story. Mercury is released when coal is burned, and much of East Asia is powered by coal-fired electrical generation plants. Wind and ocean currents carry mercury and other combustion byproducts north and eventually into the Bering Sea. The U.S. Environmental Protection Agency estimates that 100-300 tons of mercury is deposited in the Arctic with snowfall, and half that is transferred into the water cycle when the snow melts. Elevated mercury levels have been found in some ducks and falcons.

Radioactivity

Radioactive substances probably entered the basin from dumping of waste materials and from atmospheric nuclear testing. Some contamination by plutonium isotopes is believed to come from Soviet military sources that used the sea as a dump. The composition of some of the materials detected in Bering Sea sediments indicates that it was generated by atmospheric testing or by the three underground nuclear tests conducted in the late 1960s and early 1970s on Amchitka Island in the Aleutians. Atmospheric testing has been banned by treaty for decades, but radioactive substances can take thousands of years to degrade in the environment.

Human risks?

There is concern that pollutants, especially persistent organics and heavy metals, may be accumulating in the edible tissues of marine organisms that constitute important subsistence foods for Native people on the Bering Sea coasts. Testing so far has not revealed widespread health threats, although people are warned against consuming certain organs of some species. To date there is no convincing evidence that pollutants have significantly harmed the overall ecosystem of the Bering Sea.

Oil pollution

Oil drilling could become a pollution source in the Bering Sea. Fuel and oil spills from

Fuel oil is transferred from a grounded freighter at Dutch Harbor.

There are perils to humans as well as to the environment on the Bering Sea. Top—A ship loaded with logs lost some of them overboard and dangerously listed as it plowed through big swells. Bottom—The longline fishing vessel *Galaxy* burns after an explosion on the Bering Sea. Three men died, one of whom was swept overboard from a vessel that answered the *Galaxy's* Mayday call.

shipping also are threats. Already hundreds of large cargo ships transiting between North America and Asia pass through the southern Bering Sea as they take the "Great Circle Route" through the Aleutians. If the Northern Sea Route (Russia) or the Northwest Passage (Canada) become major shipping routes, hundreds more ships annually could cross the Bering Sea. Each ship represents a risk of pollution from minor intentional discharges and from major spills that could result from grounding mishaps.

Marine debris

Not all pollution is as difficult to detect as POPs and heavy metals are. Various kinds of debris drift around in the Bering Sea and wash up on its beaches.

Lost or discarded fishing gear, rope, packing materials, fuel drums, and plastic containers that previously held all sorts of household and industrial substances, litter those beaches.

Most are durable and unsightly but not otherwise harmful. However, synthetic fishing net web that can persist in the environment for many years entangles and kills fish, birds, and even mammals before it gets wrapped up and buried in the sand by wave action. Carton banding straps and similar materials sometimes strangle seals and sea lions. Some drums leak fuel, oil, or hazardous chemicals into the environment.

Other kinds of "debris" are sought-after treasures. The chance of finding whale bones and walrus tusks draws beachcombers to certain accessible locations, and many beachcombers like to collect the ubiquitous Japanese glass balls. These glass spheres were made as net floats and some apparently have ridden North Pacific and Bering Sea currents for decades before fetching up on certain sandy beaches where they may occur in the dozens or hundreds.

Fisheries challenges

Management

Fisheries management conflicts reflect social and economic

Ocean debris is a worldwide problem, and the Bering Sea has its share. Lost or jettisoned fishing lines and nets are particularly troublesome, fouling beaches and sometimes entangling wildlife, such as the northern fur seal shown in the top photo.

interests that always clash where large sums of money are involved. The U.S.-Russian disagreement over the location of the line dividing the two countries' territorial waters eventually will be settled through diplomatic negotiation. Increased cooperation between the United States and Russia is gradually improving fishery management, particularly for transboundary species like salmon and pollock.

On the other hand, Russian fisheries management is in chaos since the central government

reduced funding for management agencies. Those agencies are compelled to sell "research quotas" or engage in joint ventures with fishing companies to raise needed operating funds.

The effectiveness of some Russian fisheries management is suspect, and it is well known that since the breakup of the Soviet Union some fish stocks have been seriously overharvested. Because key stocks like Bering Sea pollock roam freely across the sea, fishery management

Bering Sea fishing operations produce staggering amounts of bycatch.

A bottom trawler hauls in a catch of groundfish from the Bering Sea in a study that assessed the effects of bottom trawling on seafloor habitat.

problems on the Russian side can harm the entire resource.

Bycatch

While sustainably harvesting valuable sea products, the fishing industry can also have deleterious effects on the ocean. Foremost are high levels of *bycatch*, and damage to the bottom habitat.

Bycatch refers to non-target fish, shellfish, and other invertebrates (and even includes birds and marine mammals) that are unintentionally caught in fishing gear. Nearly 1,000 species of sea life are taken inadvertently in Alaska's fisheries. Some bycatch consists of commercially undesirable or even legally prohibited species; others are *economic discards*, which are fish of the right species but too small to be processed profitably. For most

of the history of the fishery bycatch was simply dumped overboard. Changes in regulation now require full retention and full utilization of most bycatch, and are intended to provide disincentives to vessels that fish "dirty"—that is, produce high levels of bycatch. That doesn't mean the catch ends up as an edible product; most goes into vacuum dryers to become low-value fish meal used in fertilizers and livestock feed.

Bering Sea fishing operations produce staggering amounts of bycatch. In 1998 and 1999 about 275 million pounds (125,000 metric tons) of bycatch were taken per year by American fleets alone in the Bering Sea and Aleutian Islands, 80 to 90 percent of it by trawlers. The cod factory trawler fleet in 1999 had a discard rate of 38 percent (of

Challenges

landed weight) while the cod pot fleet discarded only 3.4 percent. Discard rates range from three percent for pot boats and 11 percent for some longline fisheries, to highs of 57 percent for other longline fisheries, and of 40, 50, and 60 percent for some bottom trawl fisheries.

A combination of measures, including a ban on bottom trawling for Bering Sea pollock, bycatch caps, full retention, and time and area closures, are getting bycatch levels down. Additional measures, including improved data gathering and conversion to "cleaner" gear like hook-and-line and traps or pots, can further reduce bycatch.

Habitat destruction

The same gear types (bottom trawls and, to a lesser extent, pelagic trawls that frequently contact the bottom) that produce the highest bycatch rates also cause the greatest damage to the seafloor. Trawls use heavy steel plates called "doors" to spread open the net, and those doors, along with cables, chains, ropes, and rollers, plow and scrape the bottom. On hard rocky bottoms the heavy gear smashes and sweeps away the corals, sponges, anemones, and other bottom life, greatly diminishing the complexity of bottom habitat which fish and crabs need to breed, feed, and rear.

Trawling over soft bottoms is less of a problem. Studies show that soft bottom areas where trawl gear is used have a low diversity of species and are dominated by opportunistic creatures like sea stars, which have no commercial value and contribute little to the food web.

Trawlers have combed nearly all of the Bering Sea shelf and slope over the years, and thousands of square miles of mostly soft bottom are swept by trawl net footropes annually. It is believed that decades are required for some kinds of damaged habitat to recover fully, and even centuries in the case of corals. Area closures and gear modification or substitution ultimately will bring about a decrease in habitat damage.

Trawl gear isn't the only culprit in bottom habitat destruction. Groundlines used by longliners often sweep the bottom as they are retrieved in areas of strong currents and waves, and hooks and gangions snag lots of coral and sponge.

Forty-square-foot, 700-pound pots can do some damage when they are dropped by the thousands onto the ocean floor. And every season, hundreds

Fishing for facts

Increasingly, scientists and fishermen alike have become interested in the impacts of bottom trawling on the seafloor habitat in the Bering Sea. Studies elsewhere in the world suggest that bottom trawling degrades fish habitat leading to a loss of species diversity.

NPMR scientists who worked with commercial fishermen to study the issue in the Bering Sea found that the impacts of bottom trawling depends on the type of bottom being fished and the nets and fishing methods being used. In areas dominated by sand and mud bottoms, soil compaction and redistribution of invertebrate species were observed, but were probably not significant considering that such areas are already impacted by large storms and currents. Conversely, bottom

Fish from the Bering Sea are emptied onto the deck of a chartered trawler in an NPMR study that examined the effects of bottom trawling on soft bottoms.

trawling impacts to areas dominated by corals, cobble, and other structures important to marine life are believed to be significant and detrimental to marine life.

A herring gillnet fisherman at Togiak.

Scientists, engineers, economists, fishermen, hunters, environmentalists, bureaucrats, and politicians all are looking for ways to understand, protect, and use the Bering Sea.

of pots are lost. The so-called "ghost fishing" pots may continue to catch crabs and fish until their plastic mesh disintegrates, which takes years. Today pots are supposed to be constructed with biodegradable mesh and trap doors with hinges that deteriorate fairly rapidly, preventing further entrapment of animals. It is not known how effective these construction methods are in reducing ghost fishing.

Even purse seine and gillnet leadlines scrape the bottom in shallow water, but the combined effects of all these gears is minimal compared to large-scale bottom trawling.

As fisheries managers turn increased attention to habitat preservation, the industry will make more effort to minimize the impacts of their operations.

Harvest allocation

Conflicts among competing harvester and processor groups for access to the fish and shell-fish resources are being fought in the North Pacific Fishery Management Council, in the courts, and by lobbyists and interest groups in Washington, D.C. In the 1990s the council began a process of assigning to individual fishermen and companies quota share rights to harvest the resources, and rights to process the catch to individual processing companies. This process eventually will make the fisheries safer for the participants by eliminating the "race for the fish," and more predictable for owners, and will ensure better financial

returns by reducing *overcapitalization*. But it will prevent new participants from entering the industry except by the purchase of quota shares from existing holders. Processor shares would compel fishermen to sell their catch to certain buyers, reducing their ability to get the best price.

Environmental groups and Native advocacy organizations are gaining increasing influence in the fishery management process and likely will shift the direction of decisions in the future. The need to meet federal standards for provision of resources to subsistence users may change the complexion of fishery management as well.

Fewer salmon

The ongoing Western Alaska economic crisis, which is rooted in geographical and cultural isolation, is exacerbated by two recent developments. One is the downturn in salmon returns to the region. Some of that may be related to interceptions of Western Alaska–bound salmon in other Alaska districts, or by foreign fleets either fishing illegally or under provisions of quotas in the extended fishery zones of other countries. But indications are that climate change and other environmental factors account for most of the effect. It is beyond the ability of humans to change the effect in the near term.

Fish value

Another big problem confronting commercial fishermen and their communities is that the value of salmon and herring in world markets has plummeted due to changing cultural and economic conditions.

In the case of salmon, the dramatic increase in the production of farm-reared fish on the market has been the driving factor by making more fish available than the market can absorb at prices fishermen need to survive and prosper. In less than two decades farmed salmon product has increased from nothing to about half of world salmon production, even at a time when wild salmon production in the North Pacific is increasing.

Complicating the salmon supply picture is the fact that much of the world's "wild" salmon supply actually originates in the fish hatcheries of the United States, Canada, Russia, and Japan. Concern is growing that this enormous release of juvenile salmon into the sea is causing two problems: (1) It is contributing to an oversupply of salmon on the market, and (2) it is causing an overgrazing of ocean pastures.

Some people believe that hatchery fish out-compete wild stocks, reducing salmon returns. This is an unproven theory, but it is known that Pacific Rim salmon hatchery production has increased dramatically in the last two decades.

Herring demand is down

The herring fishery, which during the 1980s and 1990s poured much needed cash into dozens of needy western Alaska villages, has fallen on hard times for an entirely different reason. A holiday delicacy deeply rooted in Japanese tradition, herring roe has been quite valuable on the market. But changing demographics and new buying habits of younger Japanese consumers have left herring roe a less valued product.

Coupled with a strong U.S. dollar and a general cooling of the overheated Japanese economy, this diminished appreciation of herring roe results in a demand—expressed in prices paid to fishermen—so weak that most of the herring fishermen have not been able to afford to stay in the fishery. Those who have continued to participate are receiving payments that are one-fifth or less of what they were during the heyday of the fishery.

Coping with change

Despite attempts to reverse the trend, it is unlikely that wild salmon and roe herring will regain their former value, and fishermen are going to have to learn to live with lower prices for their catch.

There are many ways to mitigate the effects of lower prices, including reducing the number of participating vessels, improving quality, and increasing harvesting efficiency.

But in the final analysis the region likely is in a transitional period and residents will have to develop new skills and find alternative ways of supporting themselves and their families.

Change is inevitable

The Bering Sea is not dying. Some obvious measures of productivity are down but overall it remains a healthy and productive environment.

The time perspective of most people, and the data sets of most research institutions, are too short to reveal the natural oscillations of climate and biological productivity that characterize all ecosystems. Losses tend to balance gains in natural systems, and the challenge to people is to adapt to the losses and capitalize on the gains. Scientists, engineers, economists, fishermen, hunters, bureaucrats, and politicians all are looking for ways to understand, protect, and use the Bering Sea.

Compared with other American landscapes and coastal zones, the Bering Sea is relatively untouched by human activity, and it holds promise of remaining intact and healing whatever wounds it has sustained. Managers have learned from the mistakes of other regions. Neighbors on the Russian side are learning from their own history and from some of the good examples being set elsewhere.

Cautious optimism

The prognosis for the future of the Bering Sea remains good, but only through vigilance and commitment to putting the long-term health of the resources above immediate economic gain will the rich potential of the sea be realized.

REFERENCES

Alaska Community Database Online. (no date). Department of Commerce and Economic Development, http://www.dced.state.ak.us/cbd/commdb/CF_COMDB.htm.

Alaska Marine Conservation Council. (No date). What is marine habitat? http://www.akmarine.org/whatishabitat.html. Alaska Marine Conservation Council, Anchorage.

Alaska Sea Grant College Program. 1993. Is It Food? Addressing marine mammal and seabird declines. Alaska Sea Grant College Program, University of Alaska Fairbanks, Fairbanks.

Alaska SeaLife Center. 2003. The Bering Sea. Ocean Chronicles 5(1). Alaska SeaLife Center, Seward.

Alexander, V. 1998. The bountiful Bering Sea. Presented at the Alaska Fisheries Lecture Series, January 14, 1998, University of Alaska Fairbanks, Marine Advisory Program, Anchorage. Unpublished.

Armstrong, R.H. 1994. Alaska's birds: A guide to selected species. Alaska Northwest Books, Anchorage.

Armstrong, R.H. 1998. Guide to the birds of Alaska. Alaska Northwest Books, Anchorage.

Banks, D., M. Williams, J. Pearce, A. Springer, R. Hagenstein, and D. Olson (eds.). 2000. Ecoregion-based conservation in the Bering Sea. The Nature Conservancy of Alaska, Anchorage.

Baskin, J.A. 2002. The Pleistocene fauna of south Texas, http://users.tamuk.edu/kfjab02/SOTXFAUN.htm. Texas A&M University, Kingsville.

Bates, R.L., and J.A. Jackson (eds.). 1984. Dictionary of geological terms. Anchor Books–Doubleday, New York.

Bennett, J. 2002. Sea otters take a nose dive. Defenders 77(1). Winter-spring issue.

Bigelow Laboratory for Ocean Sciences. (No date). Cycling through the food web, http://www.bigelow.org/bacteria. Bigelow Laboratory for Ocean Sciences, Boothbay Harbor, Maine.

Bigelow Laboratory for Ocean Sciences. (No date). Phytoplankton, http://www.bigelow.org/foodweb/microbe0.html. Bigelow Laboratory for Ocean Sciences, Boothbay Harbor, Maine, and NASA Oceanography, Washington, D.C.

Broeker, W.S. 1991. The great ocean conveyor. Oceanography 4(2).

Cacy, R.L. 2002. MMS gauges interest in proposed Norton Basin Sale. Press release, U.S. Minerals Management Service. Unpublished.

Charton, B. 2001. The facts on file dictionary of marine science. Checkmark Books, New York.

Chukotka and Sibneft News. 2002. Anadyr Basin, Russian Far East, Part I, Assessment Internet Geology News Letter No. 153, June 10, 2002, http://www.users.qwest.net/~kryopak/ChukotkaNewApril2002.html.

DeMaster, D., and S. Atkinson (eds.). 2002. Steller sea lion decline: Is it food II. Alaska Sea Grant College Program, University of Alaska Fairbanks, Fairbanks.

Dragoo, D.E., G.V. Byrd, and D.B. Irons. 2001. Breeding status, population trends and diets of seabirds in Alaska, 2000. U.S. Fish and Wildlife Service, Homer, Alaska.

Dunbar, C.O. 1960. Historical geology. John Wiley & Sons Inc., New York-Fienup-Riordan, A. 1988. The Yup'ik Eskimos as described in the travel journals and ethnographic accounts of John and Edith Kilbuck, 1885-1900. Limestone Press, Kingston, Ontario, pp. 58-59.

Gerhard, B. 2001. Beringian Notes 9(1). U.S. National Park Service.

Gibson, M.A., and S.B. Schullinger. 1998. Answers from the ice edge. Greenpeace Alaska, Anchorage.

Gray, G. 2000. Bering Sea Ecosystem Project, Final Report. Alaska Office of the Governor, Juneau.

Gray, P. 2003. Chukotka map, http://www.chukotka-ethnography.org/mappage.html. The Chukotka autonomous okrug: An ethnographic Web site.

Gualterieri, L. 2003. The extent and chronology of glaciation in the Anadyr region of Chukotka, Far Eastern Russia, http://faculty.washington.edu/lyn4/far_eastern_russia.htm. Quaternary Research Center, University of Washington, Seattle.

Hare, S.R., and N. Mantua. 2000. Empirical evidence for North Pacific regime shifts in 1977 and 1989. Progress in Oceanography 47(2-4):103-145.

Hayden, T. 2002. Fire and ice. U.S. News and World Report, May 27, 2002.

Harrington, G.A., and D. Crouse (compilers). 1998. Ecosystem-based management in the Bering Sea. Proceedings of the Alaska Seas Marine Conservation Biology Workshop, October 6-7, 1997, Anchorage, Alaska. Center for Marine Conservation, Washington, D.C.

Heifetz, J. 2000. Coral in Alaska: Distribution, abundance, and species associations. Paper presented at the First International Symposium on Deep Sea Corals, July 30-Aug. 2, 2000, Dalhousie University, Halifax, Nova Scotia, Canada.

Hood, D.W., and E.J. Kelley, (eds.). 1974. Oceanography of the Bering Sea. University of Alaska Institute of Marine Science, Fairbanks.

Huntington, H.P. (ed.). 2000. Impacts of changes in sea ice and other environmental parameters in the Arctic. U.S. Marine Mammal Commission, Bethesda, Maryland.

Jadamec, L.S., W.E. Donaldson, and P. Cullenberg. 1999. Biological field techniques for *Chionoecetes* crabs. Alaska Sea Grant College Program, University of Alaska Fairbanks, Fairbanks.

Jet Propulsion Laboratory. 1996. Everything you ever wanted to know about ice but were afraid to ask, http://southport.jpl.nasa.gov/polar/iceinfo.html. NASA Jet Propulsion Laboratory, California Institute of Technology, Pasadena.

Kizzia, T. 2003. PCB report kicks off controversy, www.adn.com/front/v-printer/story/2655041p-2697397c.html. Anchorage Daily News, February 21, 2003. Anchorage, Alaska.

Kondratyev, A.Ya., and K.D. Wohl. 1994. Beringian Seabird Bulletin. Russian Academy of Sciences and U.S. Department of the Interior.

Kramer, D.E., and V.M. O'Connell. 1995. Guide to Northeast Pacific rockfishes: Genera *Sebastes* and *Sebastolobus*. Alaska Sea Grant College Program, University of Alaska Fairbanks, Fairbanks.

Kramer, D.E., W.H. Barss, B.C. Paust, and B.E. Bracken. 1995. Guide to Northeast Pacific flatfishes: Families Bothidae, Cynoglossidae, and Pleuronectidae. Alaska Sea Grant College Program, University of Alaska Fairbanks, Fairbanks.

Levinsen, H., J.T. Turner, T.G. Nielsen, and B.W. Hansen. 2000. On the trophic coupling between protists and copepods in arctic marine ecosystems. Abstract in Marine Ecology Progress Series 204:65-77.

Li, W.K.W., and P.M. Dickie. (No date). Distribution and abundance of bacteria in the ocean, http://www.mar.dfo-mpo.gc.ca/science/review/1996/Li/Li_e.html. Fisheries and Oceans Canada, Maritimes Region, Dartmouth, Nova Scotia.

Loughlin, T., and K. Ohtani (eds.). 1999. Dynamics of the Bering Sea. Alaska Sea Grant College Program, University of Alaska Fairbanks, Fairbanks.

MacLean, D., S. Haley, and J. Larson. 1995. Description of geologic plays, 1995 National Resource Assessment, Navarin Basin Assessment Province, http://www.mms.gov/alaska/re/asmtdata/navarin/navaplay.htm. Alaska Federal Offshore, U.S. Minerals Management Service.

Mathisen, O.A., and K.O. Coyle (eds.). 1996. Ecology of the Bering Sea: A review of the Russian literature. Alaska Sea Grant College Program, University of Alaska Fairbanks, Fairbanks.

McCartney, M.S. 1994. A primer on ocean currents: Measurements and lingo of physical oceanographers. Coastal Brief 1994-05, http://www.whoi.edu/coastal-briefs/Coastal-Brief-94-05.html. Oceanus, Woods Hole Oceanographic Institution, Woods Hole, Massachusetts.

McNab, W.H., and P.E. Avers. 1994. Ecological subregions of the United States, Chapter 2, Bering tundra subregion, http://www.fs.fed.us/land/pubs/ecoregions/ch2.html. U.S. Forest Service, Publication WO-WSA-5.

Minerals Management Service. 2000. Undiscovered oil and gas resources. Alaska Federal Offshore. U.S. Minerals Management Service. December 2000 update. Unpublished.

Morgan, L. 1979. Alaska's Native people. Alaska Geographic 6(3).

Morseth, M. 1998. Puyulik Pu'irtuq! The people of the volcanoes: Aniakchak National Monument and Preserve ethnographic overview and assessment. Lake Clark and Katmai National Park and Preserve, National Park Service, Anchorage.

National Park Service. (No date). Beringian Land Bridge National Preserve, http://www.nps.gov/bela/html/where.htm. U.S. National Park Service.

National Park Service. (No date). Beringian Heritage International Park Program, http://www.nps.gov/akso/beringia/. U.S. National Park Service.

National Research Council. 1996. The Bering Sea ecosystem. National Research Council, National Academy Press, Washington, D.C.

NOAA. (No date). Coral in Alaska, http://www.afsc.noaa.gov/abl/MarFish/coral.htm. NOAA, Alaska Fisheries Science Center, Seattle.

NOAA. (No date). Sponges, http://www.afsc.noaa.gov/groundfish/HAPC/Sponges_synopsis.htm. NOAA, Alaska Fisheries Science Center, Seattle.

NOAA. (No date). The bathymetry of the Bering Sea, http://www.pmel.noaa.gov/bering/pages/bseamap2.html. NOAA, Pacific Marine Environmental Laboratory, Seattle.

NOAA. (No date). North Pacific Ocean and Bering Sea theme page, http://www.pmel.noaa.gov/bering/index.html. National Oceanic and Atmospheric Administration, Bethesda, Maryland.

NOAA. 1997. Bering Sea ecosystem: A call to action. A white paper. National Oceanic and Atmospheric Administration, Bethesda, Maryland.

NOAA. 2001. Climate and marine fisheries theme page, http://www.pfeg.noaa.gov/research/climatemarine/. NOAA, Pacific Fisheries Environmental Laboratory, Southwest Fisheries Science Center, Pacific Grove, California.

NOAA and others. 1998. Bering Sea Ecosystem Workshop Report. 2nd Bering Sea Ecosystem Workshop, June 2-3, 1998, Anchorage, Alaska, http://www.pmel.noaa.gov/bering/pages/inter-agency/. National Oceanic and Atmospheric Administration, U.S. Department of the Interior, and Alaska Department of Fish and Game.

Oceana. (No date). Oceans at risk. Alaska's deep-sea corals and sponges, http://www.oceansatrisk.com/index.cfm?fuseaction=page&page ID=514. Oceana, Washington, D.C.

Oleksa, M. 1992. Orthodox Alaska: A theology of mission. St. Vladimirs Seminary Press, Crestwood.

Overland, J. 2002. Modes of climate change for the Bering Sea. Progress report to NPMR. North Pacific Marine Research Program, University of Alaska School of Fisheries and Ocean Sciences, Fairbanks.

Overland, J.E. (compiler). 2000. Bering Sea ecosystem, http://www.pmel.noaa.gov/bering/pages/inter-agency/jeo_bse.html. NOAA, Pacific Marine Environmental Laboratory, Seattle.

PBS. 2001. Harriman Expedition retraced: A century of change, http://www.pbs.org/harriman/index.html. Public Broadcasting System.

Pearson, R.W., and M. Hermans (eds.). 1998. Alaska in maps: A thematic atlas. Alaska Geographic Society, Anchorage.

Polar Research Group. (no date). Bering Sea ice, http://faldo.atmos.uiuc.edu/CT/. The Cryosphere Today. Polar Research Group, University of Illinois.

Press, F., and R. Siever. 2001. Understanding Earth. W.H. Freeman & Co., New York.

Rennick, P. (ed.). 1999. Russian America. Alaska Geographic 26(4).

Rennick, P. (ed.). 1999. The Bering Sea. Alaska Geographic 26(3).

Ritter, H. 1993. Alaska's history. Alaska Northwest Books, Anchorage.

Romanenko, O. 1994. Birds of central Beringia. U.S. National Park Service and National Audubon Society.

Rosenbaum, P. 1999. Summary of: A.W. Trites, P. Livingston, S. Mackinson, M.C. Vasconcellos, A.M. Springer, and D. Pauly. Ecosystem change and the decline of marine mammals in the eastern Bering Sea: Testing the ecosystem shift and commercial whaling hypotheses, http://whale.wheelock.edu/archives. University of British Columbia, Fisheries Centre Research Reports 1999, Vol. 7.

Schneider, D. 2000-2001. Walrus numbers decline 01.12.00, Alaska feels the heat 06.08.01, Alaskan, Russian salmon getting smaller 11.09.01, Trawling for answers 08.17.01, Kittiwake contrast 08.03.01, Plankton bloom 04.27.01, and Fingerprinting pollock 10.19.01. Arctic Science Journeys Radio scripts, Alaska Sea Grant College Program, University of Alaska Fairbanks, http://www.uaf.edu/seagrant/NewsMedia/.

Scholl, D. 1999. Wonderments about the origin and evolution of the Aleutian–Bering Sea region, with a special look at its energy resource potential and geophysical evidence for massive deposits of methane hydrate, http://sepwww.stanford.edu/bags/Talks/9908Scholl.html. Lecture presented to the Bay Area Geophysical Society, San Ramon, California.

Sevostianov, V. 2002. Commander Islands: Nature protection and conservation, http://home.attbi.com/~mishkabear/island/booklet.htm. Commander Islands and B.C. Nature Protection and Conservation Association, Victoria, British Columbia, Canada.

Short, N.M., and R.W. Blair. 1986. Geomorphology from space, Plate V-9, The Aleutian Arc, http://daac.gsfc.nasa.gov/DAAC_DOCS/geomorphology/GEO_3/GEO_PLATE_V-9.HTML. National Aeronautics and Space Administration, Washington, D.C.

Smith, B.S., and R.J. Barnett. 1990. Russian America: The forgotten frontier. Washington State Historical Society, Tacoma.

Springer, A. 1996. Prerecruit walleye pollock, *Theragra chalcogramma*, in seabird food webs of the Bering Sea. In: NOAA Technical Report NMFS 126.

Springer, A.M., J.F. Piatt, and G. Van Vliet. 1996. Sea birds as proxies of marine habitats and food webs in the western Aleutian Arc. Fisheries Oceanography 5(1).

Stromsem, N.E. 1989. A guide to Alaskan seabirds. 2nd edn. Alaska Natural History Association, Anchorage.

Tarbuck, E.J., and F.K. Lutgens. 1999. Earth. 6th edn. Prentice-Hall, Upper Saddle River, New Jersey.

Thingstad, F. 1999. Microbial ecology lectures, http://www.miljolare.no/virtue/newsletter/00_09/curr-frede/index.php. Virtue Newsletter: Curriculum. University of Bergen, Goteborg University, and University of Maryland.

Thingstad, F. 2002. Microbial loop, http://www.uib.no/ums/magazine/updates/Loop/loop.htm. Marine Science Online Magazine. University of Bergen, Goteborg University, and University of Maryland.

Townsend, R. (ed.). 1991. Proceedings of the Conference on Shared Living Resources of the Bering Sea Region. June 5-7, 1990, University of Alaska Fairbanks, Fairbanks. U.S. President's Council on Environmental Quality, Washington, D.C.

Vance, T., and A. Macklin. 1998. What the heck is a coccolithophore? Alaska Fisherman's Journal 21(3):36.

Whitney, S.R., and A.M. Springer. 2002. Jellyfish impact on food web productivity in the southeastern Bering Sea. Report to the Pollock Conservation Cooperative Research Center, University of Alaska Fairbanks, School of Fisheries and Ocean Sciences, Fairbanks.

Witherell, D. 2001. Groundfish of the Bering Sea and Aleutian Islands Area: Species profiles 2001. North Pacific Fishery Management Council, Anchorage.

Witherell, D., and C. Coon. 2000. Protecting gorgonian corals off Alaska from fishing impacts. Poster presented at the First International Symposium on Deep Sea Corals, July 30-Aug. 2, 2000, Dalhousie University, Halifax, Nova Scotia, Canada.

World Wildlife Fund. 2002. Species spotlight: Northern fur seals. Bering Sea Ecoregion News, World Wildlife Fund, Summer/fall issue.

Wynne, K. 1997. Guide to marine mammals of Alaska. 2nd edn. Alaska Sea Grant College Program, University of Alaska Fairbanks, Fairbanks.

PERSONAL COMMUNICATIONS

Alderson, Judy, National Park Service

Alexander, Vera, SFOS, UAF

Alton, Tom, Alaska Native Language Center, UAF

Bailey, Palmer, Kenai Peninsula College

Benson, Poppy, USFWS

Braddock, Joan, Institute of Arctic Biology, UAF

Branson, Jim, Halibut Cove, Alaska

Brown, Eloise, SFOS, UAF

Burdin, Alexander, Alaska SeaLife Center

Burkanov, Vladimir, National Marine Mammal Lab, NOAA

Cailliet, Gregor, Moss Landing Marine Lab, California State University

Christensen, Doug, Geophysical Institute, UAF

Cloe, John, U.S. Air Force

Clough, James, Alaska Department of Natural Resources

Coccia, Deborah, Geophysical Institute, UAF

Cody, Mary, USFWS

Corbett, Debby, USFWS

Craig, James, U.S. Minerals Management Service

D'Amico, Jennifer, World Wildlife Fund

Feirer, Shane, The Nature Conservancy

Finney, Bruce, IMS, UAF

Fox, Lisa, USFWS

Garza, Dolly, MAP, UAF

Hagenstein, Randy, The Nature Conservancy.

Hammer, Alison, NOAA

Heifeitz, Jon, NOAA

Hia Andrews, Allen, Moss Landing Marine Lab,
    California State University

Highsmith, Ray, IMS, UAF

Hopcroft, Russell, IMS, UAF

Jack, Lianna, Alaska Sea Otter and Steller Sea Lion Commission

Jewett, Stephen, IMS, UAF

Johnson, Mark, IMS, UAF

Konar, Brenda, SFOS, UAF

Kowalik, Zygmunt, IMS, UAF

Kramer, Donald, MAP, UAF

Kromann, Sonja, NOAA

Larson, John, Minerals Management Service

Lauth, Robert, NOAA

Lingnau, Tracey, ADFG

Long, Nancy, ADFG

Marcy, Suzanne, U.S. Environmental Protection Agency

Matkin, Craig, North Gulf Oceanic Society

McRoy, Peter, IMS, UAF

Mercy, Deborah, MAP, UAF

Mitchell, Henry, Bering Sea Fisherman's Association

Ogbe, Abigail, Alaska Department of Environmental Conservation

Okkonen, Steve, SFOS, UAF

Paust, Brian, MAP, UAF

Pearson, Catherine, USFWS

Pearson, Roger, Institute of the North, Alaska Pacific University

Piatt, John, U.S. Geological Survey

Platte, Robert, USFWS

Rugh, David, NOAA

Sevostianov, Vladimir, Commander Islands Nature Protection Association

Shirley, Tom, SFOS, UAF

Smirnov, Gennady, Kaira Club, Anadyr, Russia

Smith, Stacy, SFOS, UAF

Sowls, Art, USFWS

Spencer, Paul, NOAA

Springer, Alan, IMS, UAF

Steiner, Richard, MAP, UAF

Strom, Suzanne, Western Washington University

Vyatkin, Pyotr, Kamchtka Institute of Ecology and Nature Management

Weingartner, Thomas, IMS, UAF

Wetherell, Roger, U.S. Coast Guard

Wettengel, Wesley, World Wildlife Fund

Whitledge, Terry, IMS, UAF

Williams, Margaret, World Wildlife Fund

Wilson, Matt, NOAA

Witten, Evie, The Nature Conservancy

Wyers, Abby, The Nature Conservancy

Wynne, Kate, MAP, UAF

Young, Chuck, USFWS

ADFG = Alaska Department of Fish and Game

IMS = Institute of Marine Science

MAP = Marine Advisory Program

NOAA = National Oceanic and Atmospheric Administration

SFOS = School of Fisheries and Ocean Sciences

UAF = University of Alaska Fairbanks

USFWS = U.S. Fish and Wildlife Service

INDEX

(Pages with photos or illustrations are italicized.)